G000020417

Patrick W. Byrne

Les Liaisons dangereuses :
A Study of Motive and Moral

University of Glasgow French and German Publications

University of Glasgow French and German Publications

General Editor (First Series): James A. Coleman

Consultant Editors : Colin Smethurst
Kenneth Varty

Modern Languages Building, University of Glasgow,
Glasgow G12 8QL, Scotland.

First published 1989

© Copyright University of Glasgow French and German Publications.
All rights reserved. No part of this publication may be reproduced,
stored in a retrieval system, or transmitted, in any form or by any
means, electronical, mechanical, recording or otherwise, without the
prior permission of the publisher.

Printed by Glasgow University Printing Department.

ISBN   0 85261 252 4

Contents

Acknowledgements

I should like to thank the editors of *Essays in French Literature* and *Studies on Voltaire and the Eighteenth Century* for kindly allowing me to incorporate in an adapted form as chapters in this book material which originally appeared as articles in their journals, in 1986 and 1989 respectively.

In these days of cutbacks and financial stringency, it is a privilege for me to express my gratitude to the executive committee of the Carnegie Trust for the Universities of Scotland and the British Academy for their generous publication subventions.

My grateful thanks go to Scotsys Computer Systems for preparing my text for printing.

On a personal note, I would also like to thank family, colleagues and friends, without whose help, encouragement and forbearance I could not have completed this study.

Patrick W. Byrne   Glasgow, April 1989

Acknowledgements

Problems and Preliminaries

Many of the problems which Laclos's novel raises have been successfully dealt with; some important ones remain only partly accounted for, even today, after several decades of intensive critical study. Thanks to the painstaking work of Laurent Versini we now have a definitive text of *Les Liaisons dangereuses* , illuminated with many excellent stylistic and semantic analyses, and we know a great deal about the use Laclos made of commonplace themes and motifs in the construction of his story, the literary sources and parallels it evokes, and the contemporary and later reception of the book. [1] Nor can there be much to add to, or any point in recapitulating, the various demonstrations of Laclos's development and mastery of the techniques of the epistolary form; this is a rich vein of critical exposition, yet one which now seems close to exhaustion. [2] Georges Poisson's recent book [3] has added some valuable insights to the picture of Laclos's life presented in Dard's biography, without really changing the view of Laclos's motivation in writing the novel which Poisson and other critics (Vailland, for example) have inherited from Dard. The best general guide to the interpretation of *Les Liaisons dangereuses* and its literary techniques must remain Jean-Luc Seylaz, whose study, ' *Les Liaisons dangereuses* ' *et la création romanesque chez Laclos* (Droz, 1958), still stands as a monument to the creative intelligence and sympathetic penetration of that scholarly commentator.

What problems remain may be classified into several not necessarily entirely distinct groups. Firstly the form of the text itself, or a version of it, can sometimes be misleading. [4] Then there are uncertainties which even a brief reflection on the text serves to dispel; there are those problems which have been created by the shortsightedness or over-active imagination of the exegetes; there is conjecture in areas where the evidence of the text is inconclusive, or speculation which fails to shed further light on its meaning; finally, alongside aspects of the novel which, since they have never been fully explored, might seem to, but do not in fact present problems, there are very real difficulties which derive from the hesitation of the author, the intentional polyvalence of meaning of his text, or, more accurately perhaps, from Laclos's wish to continue to make allowance for several alternative interpretations even though the individual reader may, naturally enough, have already opted for what is to him the single most plausible line of interpretation of a book which seems to tie an interpretative knot of Gordian proportions so as to invite the reader to cut it.

There will always be disagreement about the reasons for the actions of Valmont and Merteuil, the quality of their feelings, and how far it is possible—whether the attempt is worthwhile, even—to disentangle these from the play-acting in which they indulge. Critics will continue to argue endlessly about the message of the work and the implications of its ironic dénouement. But this present book makes it clear, I hope, that any solution offered to any of the central problems of exegesis of the novel—the psychology of motivation, the moral issue, and the allied question of irony and its purpose—cannot be convincing if it is based on a selective reading of Laclos's text, and that once a commitment is made to a line of explication it has to be rigorously followed through without shrinking from a clear-sighted recognition of all its consequences.

The story itself, [5] however intricate; the topicality of the novel; the credibility of events and the credentials of this collection of letters in which they are described; the kind of characters who make up this enclosed society which keeps in touch in this way—all this would not seem to be in doubt.

The novel introduces to the scene two rival libertines: Valmont, whose name perhaps evokes his libertine energy and the ubiquity of his seductive presence ('par monts et par vaux') as much as it does his contradictory tendencies to 'high' sensibility or 'low' sensuality; and Merteuil, the all-seeing ('œil') hammer ('martel') of the male sex, whose acquaintance or influence is so deadly to the Vicomte and to Mme de Tourvel ('mortel'; 'cercueil'), and who, in her role as mentor to Cécile substitutes for Mme de Volanges ('mère'). [6] These two libertines plan revenge, and indeed the whole plot could be described as a series of variations on this theme. There is Merteuil's revenge on her ex-lover Gercourt through the corruption of Cécile, a plan which is ultimately foiled since Cécile does not marry. (At one point this strategy entails a subsidiary revenge on Danceny for failing as the instrument of primary vengeance: see L.54, F150, and L.63, F167.) There is Valmont's revenge on Mme de Volanges, through her daughter, for warning Tourvel against him; and there is his implacable victimisation of Mme de Tourvel, whose seduction amounts to the retaliation of a libertine against Virtue personified ("vertu", and the English "True Love" are approximate anagrams of her name). [7] Finally there is the settling of accounts in the *Compte ouvert entre la Marquise de Merteuil et le Vicomte de Valmont* (L.169, F460): the mutual revenge of the two rivals for the humiliating preference each has for another less 'worthy' partner (see F336 and F387-8), an outcome which appears inevitable when they run short of victims other than themselves.

How topical is *Les Liaisons dangereuses* , and more specifically, how up-to-date is the reader of the time encouraged to believe it is ? There are one or two hints that the reader in 1782 is meant to recognise that this correspondence has dated somewhat. For example, it would appear to be intended that he should assume from the footnote to L.169 that the letters were not released for publication until after the death of

Mme de Rosemonde; similarly, the comment in the footnote in L.6 on 'le mauvais goût des calembours, qui commençait à prendre, et qui depuis a fait tant de progrès' (F45) creates a certain distancing effect. And yet 'calembour' is a neologism which J. Papadopoulos says is first attested in a letter of Diderot in 1786 (F486). The *earliest* the events of the novel could be dated by the contemporary reader is 1768-69: there are brief passing references to events in Corsica in those years in L.9, F52 and L.111, F323 (see the Versini ed., p.1190, n. 5) which can easily be overlooked. Alongside references to the Présidente's unfashionable 'panier' in L.5, [8] to 'ce rôle de confident, contre lequel il s'est établi des préjugés' (L.63, F170), [9] and to the 'vieux Ministre' in L.81, F229, [10] this suggests that the events recounted in the letters could be presumed to have happened any time between 1768 and *1780* . There can be no doubt about the topicality of the novel. In the 'Avertissement de l'éditeur', it is remarked of the author:

> En effet, plusieurs des personnages qu'il met en scène ont de si mauvaises mœurs, qu'il est impossible de supposer qu'ils aient vécu dans notre siècle de philosophie, où les lumières, répandues de toutes parts, ont rendu, comme chacun sait, tous les hommes si honnêtes et toutes les femmes si modestes et si réservées. (F25)

This antiphrastic irony entirely lacks thrust unless Laclos considers he is mirroring the persistent depravities of the age. At times Laclos may be grasping at straws when, under attack after publication for his "scandalous" work, he defends his novel from the point of view of its contemporary relevance and the true-to-life accuracy of its character portrayal, [11] and yet there has to be a basis of credibility in the whole argument for him ever to have thought of using it. *Libertinage* may have been a little out of fashion in 1782, [12] and in employing irony as its chief mode *Les Liaisons dangereuses* , published in that year, may have been out-of-date tonally and stylistically because of the rise of sensibility, but here was a book which, disregarding fashion, must still have been topical in its subject matter. Jean Fabre assures us that *Les Liaisons dangereuses* was found shocking because it offended current literary tastes:

> Si Laclos en son temps a fait scandale, c'est parce qu'il a délibérément heurté ses lecteurs en renouant avec un tour d'esprit et une façon d'écrire que son époque au moins en littérature, ne goûtait ou ne comprenait plus. [13]

It can be argued that it was more shocking because it took the lid off a hypocritical society whose members attacked the novel, not because they did not want to be reminded of past faults, but because they refused to recognise the truth of the picture of their prevailing vices. Laclos had touched a raw nerve...

In this story of libertines and their revenge, some allusions in some letters and some details of parts of the plot may initially seem problematic; some critics [14] certainly contrive to make others appear so. What, for instance, are the 'secrets' that the Marquise communicates to Mme de Volanges, as mentioned in L.31 (F95) ?—obviously some revelations and warnings about Valmont to the woman who is the Présidente's mentor, for Merteuil is playing a double game. [15] What special service does Merteuil perform for Valmont (L.63, F170) which allows him to go back to Mme de Rosemonde's château after his enforced exile (Ll.43-44), when he is apparently in possession of an invitation from Rosemonde to Mme de Volanges (end of L.44) so that he can in fact himself influence Volanges's visit and create his own cover for his return to Tourvel ? (Perhaps Valmont delays conveying the invitation himself because he wants to arrange his revenge on Mme de Volanges in Paris.) If it is Merteuil who is seen to take the initiative in the invitation to Volanges, Merteuil who provides moral reinforcements on the spot for Mme de Tourvel in the person of that worthy lady and her daughter, Valmont can return to his aunt's home without it appearing that the arrangement is an elaborate plan he has himself devised; without the intervention of the "virtuous" Marquise Valmont's use of cover would be too obvious, though from the Présidente's point of view the Vicomte is still taking unfair advantage. Laclos perhaps originally planned to include a letter from Tourvel to Valmont written at some point after the seduction (see F494-5). Where would it have been placed within the collection, [16] and what is it hinting at when it breaks off ? Perhaps the letter would have come somewhere between L.132 and some roughly projected version of L.135. Probably it would have been dated 'Paris, ce 14 novembre'. 'Depuis l'instant où vous vous êtes éloigné de moi' (F494) and 'Au moment même où vous êtes sorti' (F495) bring to mind a phrase of L.138: 'je laissai là ma Belle, toute surprise' (F396). It is conceivable that Laclos originally wished to engineer some ironic clash between the Présidente's anxiety about sinning against love (perhaps on the occasion of the unexpected return of her husband claiming his conjugal rights ?) and Valmont's heedless escapade with Emilie. Belaval seems to think that this unfinished, suppressed letter, F494-5, was leading up to a confession of masturbation, [17] whereas Coulet, less grotesquely, remarks:

> La faute qu'elle a commise, c'est probablement d'avoir pleuré et prié, d'avoir un instant eu honte devant Dieu et renié sa passion coupable.[18]

At a later stage, Laclos hit upon a simple and poignant expedient for having Tourvel informed of Valmont's infidelity (F396-7) and decided to shorten the programme of events for the Présidente's evening of 14 November.

Even more problematic is the note which Laclos perhaps thought of having Valmont write to Mme de Volanges (L.155 O.S., F493-4) requesting Volanges to deliver a letter of his to Mme de Tourvel (now gravely ill after his final desertion) and to assure Tourvel of his love.

Was this suppressed because the Vicomte's true motivation appeared too clearcut—or because it seemed too ambiguous ? (This latter, surely?)[19] Does Merteuil, as evidence of Valmont's treachery to Danceny, show the young man L.158, or L.96 (see L.162) ? Critics may come to different conclusions, [20] but it hardly matters; the important thing is that she has overplayed her hand. What sequel to the novel, mentioned in the final footnote (F474), could Laclos have possibly devised, when Cécile is safely ensconced in a convent and when Merteuil's punishment already seems complete ? Delon thinks that this final note, which Fabre mistakenly assumes to be by Laclos himself, only increases the reader's uncertainty, but since the evidence of the MS suggests it cannot be attributed to Laclos the problems it raises need not concern us. [21]

Critics even disagree about the particular part of Emilie's anatomy on which Valmont supposedly wrote his famous Letter 48. Barbara Guetti insists that the 'pupitre' (F136) was her (Emilie's, that is) behind; [22] Peter Gay, on the other hand, seems to have a firmer grip of things when he writes of Valmont 'using his mistress's back as a desk'.[23] A brief consideration of the practicalities of the matter leads us to conclude that Monnet's spirited interpretation of the scene 'sans doute pour l'édition de 1796' [24] strikes the right balance between Devéria's 1820 version [25] and that of Guetti. This whole episode now brings us to the more fundamental question of the *vraisemblance* of *Les Liaisons dangereuses* .

By and large, and given the complications of the letter novel form, Laclos is very successful in displaying, arranging, and motivating his letters in a convincing form. We soon understand that since Valmont and Merteuil are such inveterate egoists, offending normal standards and intent on pursuing private plans, they need to have a private correspondence to seek approval for their values, to create themselves as characters and mythologise their roles, to comment and analyse with perverse wit and elegance, to sustain each his own vanity and self-respect, and to comment on each other's manipulative skills. Since they are ex-lovers and rival libertines they will obviously enjoy playing on, exploiting or exposing, their respective weaknesses. Cécile as a young girl who has just left the convent, ignorant of the ways of society and on the point of taking a major step in her life (or rather having it taken for her, F36), will need a confidante and a link with the world she has just left (Sophie Carnay), and her naive character will, naturally enough, express itself formally in a loose style which lacks logical articulation. Danceny will need a channel for his new-found emotions and a confidant (Valmont, ironically); as a poet he will incline to a certain kind of rhetoric and demonstrate a predilection for a rather fossilised formulaic language of love. Quite naturally enough it will be Mme de Volanges, who has arranged the Présidente's marriage, who will write to Mme de Tourvel warning her against Valmont, and, again convincingly, the conventional Volanges will be impressed by spurious moralistic arguments from Mme de Merteuil and fail to remove her daughter from danger (L.104), just as later she will fail to rise above her sense of *bienséance* and rescue Tourvel by following Valmont's suggestions (L.154, and F493). The Présidente will be forced to change her preceptress from the moralistic Mme de Volanges to the more understanding Mme de Rosemonde when she realises that she has fallen in love with the very man she was warned against. Similarly Cécile will be obliged to change confidante when seduced (L.75 and L.97). Mme de Rosemonde's rheumaticky arm (L.112) will be a convenient and convincing excuse for an artfully-placed delayed letter (L.126), arriving too late with maximum irony. The servants, being servants, will speak when they are spoken to and write when they are written to, expressing themselves in a style close to incorrectness (L.107). Generally speaking, then, we understand how these characters come to write the letters that they do write to the particular correspondents of their choice, at the time, for the reasons, in the way, and with the effect that they choose or are guided to choose.

Though in the normal run of things *Les Liaisons dangereuses* does not offend the "credibility criteria" identified by critics such as Vivienne Mylne, it is when we look at the detail that the holes begin to appear in the fabric and improbabilities seem to multiply. The chronology and the dating of some letters are uncertain despite Laclos's modification of his text. [26] Errors such as those on which Thelander comments cannot be explained as the mistakes of the "rédacteur" arranging the letters in order (cf. 'replacer par ordre les Lettres que j'ai laissé subsister', F27), for it is not a question of wrong order, but of chronology which simply will not work. However they might in turn themselves explain the phrase in the 'préface' about 'les fautes qui s'y trouvent dans les détails' (F29)—an acknowledgement kept in by Laclos perhaps because he saw it as a very necessary precaution. Moreover, with Danceny being, especially early in the novel, apparently so naive and uncalculating, there is perhaps a certain *invraisemblance* in his writing Cécile a letter in which he asks 'Et qu'ai-je à vous dire, que mes regards [...] ne vous aient dit avant moi?' (L.17) before he has even indulged in the meaningful looks to which he refers (see L.16: 'mais, toutes les fois qu'il me regardait, cela me serrait le cœur'). In L.110 Valmont says 'je la [sc. Cécile] laissai seule trois heures plus tôt que *de coutume* ' (F321, my italics), yet this is only his second encounter with her. [27] Raymond Lemieux makes the valid point that:

> Si, par exemple, la fausse couche de Cécile, quelque sept semaines après avoir passé la nuit avec Valmont la première fois, est acceptable, il est invraisemblable que celui-ci ait pu deviner sa grossesse dès le 19 octobre. [28]

Cécile only confides the news of her seduction to the Marquise on 1 October. Valmont thinks of finding out 'si la guérison était parfaite'

9

(L.144, F410) a week after the miscarriage: on the one hand his account of the girl's quick recovery looks like nothing more than a distortion to justify a provocative indirect reference to Merteuil's age (F409); on the other hand, we are invited to believe, on the evidence of her mother, that Cécile is 'presque rétablie' (F418) within nine days. Cécile has the accident on 20 November, yet despite her recent experience is seemingly prepared to welcome Danceny to her bed on 5 December (L.157). Is it likely that the young Volanges would have had the diligence to keep copies of 'cette Correspondance journalière'—her idle chatter with Sophie Carnay—and why should her mother, presumably, give these particular letters to Mme de Rosemonde ? Why would Danceny (L.169) need to hand over to Rosemonde any letters other than L.96 or L.158 to prove that he was justified in challenging Valmont to a duel, and why, and when precisely, did he give Rosemonde copies of his love letters to Merteuil, instead of destroying them in a rage at his own gullibility ? [29]

But, to be fair, these are not the sort of details that the average reader bothers about or even notices, and not the kind of questions he asks, any more than he really cares about, say, the "Moslem chronology" of the *Lettres Persanes* with which Montesquieu and some critics are preoccupied. He is simply happy to register *en passant* (L.165, L.169) that the fiction is beginning fictitiously to justify itself, for the letters are being gathered into the hands of one person, just as the chickens are coming home to roost in a figurative sense: nemesis, tautologically speaking, is overtaking the characters with a vengeance. It is no less unreasonable over-rigorously to apply the standards of nineteenth-century Realism to *Les Liaisons dangereuses* than it is to over-emphasise the reflexivity of the novel first noted by Todorov and Roelens.[30] What is much more important to the non-literal-minded is that the opening two prefaces (F25-31) apparently contradict each other, the punishment meted out to Merteuil at the end seems heavy-handed and unbelievably providential, and the book seems to degenerate into a parodically edifying moral fable which intentionally abandons *vraisemblance* to mock the reader. It is to such questions as these that my chapter on the moral of the work addresses itself.

What, then, of the characters ? What kind of creatures are these ? Are the real sexual proclivities of the Marquise and the Vicomte as problematical as their relationship apparently is ?

It is irritating for the critics constantly to assure us [31] that Valmont and Merteuil are homosexual when they manifest such a healthy appetite for the opposite sex. The evidence of the text certainly has to be taken into account. Setting aside the different social status of the characters and the general restraint of Laclos's writing, Cécile's response to Merteuil's apparent inclination and the behaviour which the Marquise encourages (L.20, F72; L.39, F115; L.54, F151; and L.55, F153) may perhaps remind us of the first steps in the sexual initiation of John Cleland's Fanny Hill. [32] Can we say of Merteuil what Fanny says of Mrs Phoebe Ayres ?

> Not that she hated men or did not even prefer them to her own sex; but when she met with such occasions as this was, a satiety of enjoyments in the common road, perhaps to a secret bias, inclined her to make the most of pleasure wherever she could find it, without distinction of sexes. [33]

Is Merteuil's apparent lesbianism a consequence of her having adopted the masculine role of the rake and become a pseudo-man herself ? Or, angry still with Gercourt, is not her real concern simply to do some preliminary pimping for Cécile so as to arouse the Vicomte's interest (for she despairs of Danceny) with predictable results for her revenge on the careless lover who preceded Valmont (cp. F169 and F320—'pénitente')? Dropping the strongest possible hint to Valmont,[34] she says:

> jamais personne ne fut plus susceptible d'une surprise des
> sens. Elle est vraiment aimable, cette chère petite! *Elle*
> *méritait un autre Amant*.... (L.54, F151; my italics)

Moreover, it is surely preposterous to draw a comparison between Valmont and Merteuil in this matter in the way that Aldridge does when he comments that:

> de profondes tendances homosexuelles, refoulées, mais
> néanmoins apparentes se trouvent chez la Marquise (XX et
> LVIII [*sic*]) et il y a trace de la même caractéristique chez
> Valmont (LXXII, le baiser de Vressac). [35]

Surely Vressac's kiss gives Valmont pleasure because he is being thanked for bringing the two lovers together when in fact, that night, he had been the cause of keeping them apart ? There is no hint of a homosexual interest; it is merely ironic amusement at being congratulated by the very man he has duped.

A subject of more fruitful debate is the problem of the central relationship between Valmont and Merteuil, the mental assumptions which lie behind it and which dictate their responses and therefore the turn of events. Michel Delon (*op. cit.*) has explored more perceptively than any other critic the opaqueness and deceitfulness of the correspondence and the uncertainties of the novel. One consequence of assuming that ambiguity is all-pervasive, however, is that there is little incentive to offer fresh insights or a committed new interpretation; it is only marginal technicalities which appear to be worth commenting on. In my chapter on the relations between the two protagonists an attempt is made to chart a middle course between, on the one hand, the methodological reductionism of Henri Duranton, [36] which, though producing interesting results, seems a little excessive in its denial of the emotional perspective, and, on the other, the excesses of what might be termed the Romantic school of Laclos criticism, [37] in which a fertile imagination may lead to not entirely convincing guesses at 'le dessous des cartes' (in Duranton's memorable phrase), in particular to assumptions about Merteuil's real feelings which cannot be properly verified from the text. Such assumptions all too readily call for the reconstruction of a sub-text of quite iceberg-like proportions: true, this tends to be produced by *any* critical approach, and it cannot be claimed that the approach in this book does not do that, but they are contradicted by one of the few statements from the author about his novel which, seen as a shrewd particularised character assessment rather than as part of a general post-rationalised defence, we are perfectly happy to trust. For Laclos himself described Merteuil to Mme Riccoboni in Letter IV of his correspondence with her about *Les Liaisons dangereuses* as 'un coeur incapable d'amour'. While we may not agree with Belaval's view of 'l'intrépidité avec laquelle les deux complices ne se cachent rien', while we may doubt his assurance 'encore ces complices ne se mentent-ils pas l'un à l'autre', [38] conversely how can we be sure, like Duranton, that all is lies, all is pretence, all is mask in 'cette trame entrecroisée de mensonges' which is their correspondence ? [39] The description "lies" is fair comment as regards those letters where the libertines manipulate their victims, for we have other letters from which to draw comparisons in order to reach the truth, letters which reveal the "lies" of L.87 or L.104, for example. But in the private correspondence of Valmont and Merteuil, outside of which there are no points of comparison as a touchstone of the truth, how can we be sure that all is lies posturing and mask, any more than that all is true, or even granted that all cannot be true ?

The participation that Laclos requires from his reader is precisely that he should determine the proportions of truth and lies, concealment, pretence, bluff and double bluff on no other basis but that of the letters themselves. If and when the mask slips, and how far calculation is abandoned in the heat of the moment (as, humanly speaking, it must sometimes be, unless we are dealing with genuine robots of self-control) is something which the reader must determine for himself from an assessment of the emotional state of the interlocutors, for when passions are high, real feelings show through and the mask is dropped. An intuitive gamble on the reader's part, an attempt to dominate the text and penetrate its ambiguity is called for, and it is perhaps no less dangerous than that gamble indulged in by the protagonists in the final throes of their struggle for domination. But it is not a gamble taken as a stab in the dark, with nothing to go on; there is no need to 'rêve[r] d'un instrument d'analyse stylistique qui déterminerait exactement le dosage du mensonge, de la vérité et de l'illusion dans chaque lettre'; [40] we have such a device in our sensitivity to the style of the letters, and another in our alertness to the overall pattern and consistency of argument and inference. Essentially my own interpretation of the Valmont-Merteuil relationship, as expressed in their exchange of letters, amounts to allowing Valmont, but not Merteuil, feelings other than vanity, and to assuming that the only way we can explain Valmont's letters to the Marquise after L.125 and the ineptitude of his mishandling of their liaison is to presuppose an initial misjudgement on his part about her "secret feelings" for him.

No apologies are offered for a presentation which gives Valmont and Merteuil a separate imaginative life in the mind of the reader, outside the correspondence they exchange but based on it: readers capable of a fresh response to a book feel quite at ease with such constructs which, when tested against the evidence of the text, enable the subtleties of Laclos's exploration of the human psyche to emerge.

Issues such as *vraisemblance* , the state of mind, feelings and motivation of the characters, their view of each other and themselves and the consequences of this, the meaning of particular allusions and episodes in the plot, the topicality of the novel—these can only be determined from a close study of the text. Is there no other way of revealing the work's significance but this? Are we justified in dissecting *Les Liaisons dangereuses* as if it were a corpse, without reference to the whole living corpus of his writings, and in a vacuum of morgue-like clinical purity ? Are there links between the fiction he wrote and the facts of Laclos's life and experience, or between the novel and the rest of his *œuvre* , which are worth studying? Does the social background against which the book was written throw light on the author's intentions and the work's significance ? What of Laclos's own statements on this, his favourite brainchild?

It is a reasonable inference that a man who wrote a novel, even in 1782, wanted to write a novel and not a political tract. [41] Why do none of the biographers invent a theory about "Laclos and the consolations of literature" instead of repeating Dard's old thesis about a man who assembled, out of frustrated ambition, a 'boulet rouge', [42] 'a bomb against the Ancien Régime' ? In 'De la guerre et de la paix', speaking with the benefit of hindsight, Laclos includes 'une immoralité profonde que la cour ne prenait même plus le soin de cacher' among 'tous ces maux et toutes ces fautes [qui] avaient rendu presque unanime le désir d'une révolution.' [43] But the fact that *Les Liaisons dangereuses* should be the satirical attack of a 'moraliste' ironically aware of the corruption and hypocrisy around him is not a proof that his book has any revolutionary overtones. There are no reliable documents to prove what Laclos's political intentions were, and even if we had any such we would still have the problem of how far and how successfully he fulfilled his stated objectives. For every time he spoke or wrote directly or indirectly about his novel his general aim was to give a post-rationalised defence of it, and we cannot even be sure that he said some of the things he is supposed to have said about it. [44] There are no work notes, either; only the variants of the MS. [45] The links between Laclos's life and his intentions in writing *Les Liaisons dangereuses* are no more certain than the links between the novel and its characters and aristocratic figures in the actual eighteenth-century world. A satire does not have to be a 'roman à clés'. Does Mme Castel-Çagarriga's impressive accumulation of circumstantial evidence pinpointing the likely models in Grenoble society [46] actually help us to make sense of or appreciate the novel better, in any case ? Do we see more merit in Laclos's portrait of Mme de Merteuil from knowing that he probably loved and hated a woman who actually existed ? [47] Does a study of *literary* parallels and sources in the works of other authors, any more than the search for real-life models, throw any light on the particular problems of interpretation arising from the text of *Les Liaisons dangereuses* ?

The precise connections between Laclos's other works and his novel are both meagre in number and not especially revealing. The criticism of Danceny by Merteuil (L.38, F113) recalls the moral of the *conte* 'Le Bon Choix' (Versini ed., pp. 555-9). In L.46 Danceny uses the expression 'talisman de l'amour': a similar phrase occurs in Laclos's later correspondence with his wife,[48] and, in this case, it is interesting to note that since the footnote—'Ceux qui n'ont pas eu l'occasion de sentir quelquefois le prix d'un mot, d'une expression, consacrés par l'amour, ne trouveront aucun sens dans cette phrase' (F134)— commenting on the sentence in Danceny's letter (L. 46) in which the expression is to be found is apparently not in the MS, it must be a last-minute addition by the Laclos who had met and loved Marie-Soulange Duperré, his future wife,[49] which places us right at the turning point of Laclos, the Janus-faced parodist-cum-panegyrist of sensibility. [50] Part of 'Les Souvenirs—Epître à Eglé', Versini ed., p. 547, foreshadows the ironic image of Cécile begging forgiveness from her "father-confessor" Valmont (L.110, F320), but this is purely coincidental. 'Des femmes et de leur éducation' mentions 'l'état de guerre perpétuelle' between women and men in the social state (Versini ed., p.422) and thus continues the theme of the war of the sexes (see

Versini ed., L.125, p.293, and his note 2, p.1357). In the 'Troisième essai' on women's education, Laclos, the family man, speaks in favour of the guided reading of novels by young ladies (Versini ed., p.440). Working backwards from this part of this later work, written between 1795 and 1799, to the 'Préface du rédacteur' of *Les Liaisons dangereuses* (F30 provides a point of comparison) would be a mistake, for it might lead us to take the moralising of the 'préface' at face value, whereas Laclos uses the device of the pompous editor to alienate the reader and force him to discover for himself (or herself) the deeper moral of the novel. [51] For an excellent exploration of the problems created by the contamination of sources and a lucid account of the conflicting emphases of Laclos's treatises on the education of women, readers should consult Jean Bloch's article in *French Studies* , 1984. [52] However, in this survey of works which postdate the novel, Bloch produces no convincing evidence of their relevance in any crucial way to an interpretation of *Les Liaisons dangereuses* .

*****

It follows from the above that the intention in this present book is to approach the text on its own terms and to judge it on its own merits. The main burden of the interpretation is to be found in the chapters on the central relationship and the message of the novel. The section on ʳony illustrates the normal mode of invention of the author and his ʳuthors, and gives additional support to the thesis of the chapter on the ʳoral. The novel's structure, too, presents few special problems of ʳnderstanding or interpretation, but no less than the more extensively ʳxplored subject of Laclos's epistolary technique, it provides a fine ʳxample of his masterful handling of detail and intricate workmanship, ʳe opportunity to observe which has not been missed. Leaving aside ʳaclos's treatises on women's education, written after the publication of *Les Liaisons dangereuses* , and not, one would think, a reliable guide to a piece of fiction, [53] I have added a brief note on the feminist viewpoint (always a fruitful topic for a tutorial), taking elements of often very divergent critical opinions and attempting to assemble a reasonably succinct pattern of argument on a subject which sometimes lends itself to very diffuse treatment. Also included in this final chapter is a review of Stephen Frear's recent film, *Dangerous Liaisons*.

'Yet another book on Laclos...' The only justification for this one, finally, could be that it has concentrated on the real problems and asked the right questions. I hope it has given, or by provoking disagreement generated, rational answers, or, at the very least, persuaded someone to take a hard look at the text for the first time.

Moral

Pictor acer vitii... (phrase from the epitaph on Laclos's tomb)

Ce dénouement sans moralité ne vaut pas mieux que le reste.
(La Harpe)

No doubt ignorant of the opinion of those French doctors who believed that the reading of novels by women could produce attacks of the "vapours", the bishop of Pavia, in conversation with Laclos, said he thought *Les Liaisons dangereuses* was a very moral work and recommended reading for young women; to Marcel Proust it was the most incredibly depraved book every written. In an exchange of letters with Mme Riccoboni following publication of the work, Laclos defended its moral purpose and orthodoxy, yet on a later occasion in conversation with Comte Alexandre de Tilly (an unreliable witness in Delmas's view) apparently implied that he wrote it to create a stir. Modern critical opinion is divided, naturally enough, between those who believe Laclos's intention was truly moral and those who are more sceptical. Attention frequently centres on the opening prefaces and the ending, and the accompanying question of irony and its purpose.

In the opening definitions of his critique of Fanny Burney's *Cecilia*, Laclos wrote:

> Si l'Histoire et le Théâtre ne peuvent nous donner qu'une connaissance imparfaite de l'homme, il faut donc la chercher dans les Livres de morale; mais si les Romans ne peuvent être généralement compris dans cette classe, quelques-uns au moins ont prouvé que c'était uniquement la faute des Auteurs, et non celle du génie; et ceux-là seulement méritent de nous occuper. Considérés sous cet aspect, ils ont droit à l'indulgence, disons mieux à l'estime

du Public, et par le bien qu'ils peuvent faire, et par le talent
qu'ils exigent.

The contention of this chapter is that *Les Liaisons dangereuses* is,
quite simply, such a 'Livre de morale', and that the insight into human
behaviour which it offers is certainly far from "imperfect". The method
used will be a close sifting of the text taking account, where
appropriate, of the critics, not least the earlier ones, who were much
preoccupied with the moral, and liable to allow their interpretation of
this, to them the only real issue, to colour their whole attitude to the text
and its author. The various arguments which can be proposed will be
assembled or reviewed, revealing the underlying moral behind the
packaging of superficial moralising, the intention being to take a fresh
look at the 'Préface du rédacteur' and at the end pages of the novel. As
a general rule, retrospective analogies working from later writings of
Laclos will be eschewed as these are never totally convincing.[1]

The first place to look is the obvious one. The two prefaces which
precede the text are both written by Laclos, being both found in the
MS. The 'Avertissement de l'éditeur' starts with a satirical dig at the
convention of introductions where authors assert that what follows is a
real-life true account of real events and people, an actual diary, or
whatever: 'nous avons [...] de fortes raisons de penser que ce n'est
qu'un Roman' (F25). But this innocent-looking literary irony soon
turns to mordant moral irony in the rest of the 'Avertissement'. Laclos
is not suggesting that his work does not ring true and that characters
like these do not exist in his day and age, because he hopes by this
disclaimer to escape criticism that his book is depraved and sets a bad
example. By antiphrasis he addresses his contemporary readers: 'Look
around you, look into your own hearts and you will see that people
nowadays in this corrupt century *do* have the same tendencies as
Valmont and Merteuil; this picture is close to the truth!' The

unexpressed corollary must be clear enough: provided that the eighteenth-century audience can recognise the truth and see its face in the mirror, it should be able to correct its faults of malicious intelligence and unprincipled behaviour. While the portrait of the libertines is 'true to the age', the picture offered of Cécile and the Présidente is, if anything, not harsh enough, the 'Avertissement' concludes. In the real world Cécile would have married despite everything, and the Présidente would have consoled herself with a new lover. If the eighteenth-century reader can recognise that in the equivalent situation in real life people would be more shameless and morally irredeemable than they are in the book, then the artificial ending of *Les Liaisons dangereuses* is morally justified since it reveals an unpalatable truth by contrast. [2]

A man who is nothing more than a *rédacteur* cannot be held responsible for any deficiency in the moral message of a book that he has merely "arranged". But the editorship is not simply a device to enable the author to sidestep censure. The subtitle appears to identify Laclos (or at any rate a certain 'M. C.... de L...') as the man who has "collected" these letters 'dans une société / et [qui les a] publiées *pour l'instruction de quelques autres'* (F23; my italics), an "editor" who makes certain moral claims for the book in his 'préface du rédacteur'.

Firstly let us accept and review these claims on a literal level.

> Il me semble au moins que c'est rendre un service aux mœurs, que de dévoiler les moyens qu'emploient ceux qui en ont de mauvaises pour corrompre ceux qui en ont de bonnes, et je crois que ces Lettres pour / ront concourir efficacement à ce but. (F29-30)

The book is a morally useful exposé of the techniques of the two libertines, putting the general public on its guard against methods typical of this well-known type. The opinions, the standards and behaviour, the ingenuity of these malevolent intellects—such things may be disturbing initially but ultimately morally justified from that viewpoint. *Les Liaisons* also illustrates the "important truth" that 'toute femme qui consent à recevoir dans sa société un homme sans mœurs, finit par en devenir la victime' (F30). This is a reference to the Présidente in her dealings with Valmont. While we, the readers, might object that we are more interested in the psychological study of a passionate woman than in any simple moral point about her fate, there can be no counter-argument on moral grounds. No matter how admirable is the Présidente's self-sacrifice (L.165, F451), no matter how sublime she is in her tragic fate, however considerable the failings of her spiritual advisers (cf. L.123), there can be no question that what we are being offered is an example to avoid, not to follow. The other 'vérité importante' is that 'toute mère est au moins imprudente, qui souffre qu'un autre qu'elle ait la confiance de sa fille' (*ibid* .). Mme de Volanges is the mother in the book who exemplifies this maxim, for it is her coldness towards her daughter that makes Cécile seek the advice of Mme de Merteuil, who first of all encourages her love for Danceny, and then actively contributes to Valmont's corruption of the girl (L.63 and L.105); ironically it is Merteuil herself who points this out (F168), for it is the immoralists who make the best moralists. 'Les jeunes gens de l'un et de l'autre sexe', the "editor" continues, 'pourraient encore y apprendre que l'amitié que les personnes de mauvaises mœurs paraissent leur accorder si facilement, n'est jamais qu'un piège dangereux, et aussi fatal à leur bonheur qu'à leur vertu' (F30): a clear allusion to Cécile's friendship with Merteuil or Danceny's with Valmont, which lead, in an exemplary way, to a loss of innocence.

But is Laclos really only interested in anticipating and answering the doubts and objections of a disturbed and totally conventional audience ? Should we accept at face value everything the "editor" says ? [3] Through the contrivance of a supposed "rédacteur" Laclos emphasises the moral lessons his work teaches, but he does this finally in such a loaded way with parodic excessive caution (F30) that one begins to suspect him of the kind of irony which is impossible to square with the moral irony of the 'Avertissement de l'éditeur'. It would be dangerous to assume, however, that the presence of irony in the 'Préface' is intended to alert the reader to Laclos's actual approval of libertine values, and distaste for all morals (in both senses of the word). Laclos's irony is a protest against the received wisdom, the pure literary convention, that novels should have all too easily identifiable moral purposes; this convention he mocks by over-emphasising the banal moral message of his book. The irony applies to bellettrists' assumptions about the reader's lack of intelligence, inability to interpret for himself, and susceptibility to corruption. It is as if Laclos was saying to himself: 'Well, if the reader wants a *simple* message in case he's led astray, as we poor writers of novels nowadays are all forced to suppose he does, then there it is—he's well and truly got one!' Again, is he perhaps satirically making fun of those *bien-pensant* readers who need to hold to such simplistic interpretation in order to soothe their conscience-stricken feelings about reading that which they stupidly fancy to be a dangerously erotic, morally subversive work? If we think we can see, behind the mask of the pompous "editor", the ironic author devaluing and distancing himself from the superficial morality of the book by putting exaggerated emphasis upon it, then this is surely an invitation to us to look, in the novel, for a more cogent account of moral values, of the passions and their influence on men and their endeavours, in the society of Laclos's time. What then begins to emerge from *Les Liaisons* is a deeper and more savage morality in tune with the witty but essentially misanthropic note struck by the "éditeur" in his opening remarks. It is a moral which underlines the inconsistency and blind complacency of all those who (following the "rédacteur") make moral judgements in a non-self-reflective way; the moral equivocalness of a society where hypocrisy, double standards, and duplicity are rife; the equal and opposite dangers of governing one's life by pure emotion or not so pure intellect; and the destructive effects of passion and pride.

*****

Let us now begin to illustrate and examine the various features of this moral we have just sketched out. Beyond the introductory prefaces and within the text of *Les Liaisons* itself, two main areas for discussion stand out: the attack on hypocrisy, and the interpretation of the dénouement.

Firstly let us consider three aspects of hypocrisy. The first point concerns the sexual double standard.

At the end of L.27, in her naivety, Cécile unknowingly manages to convey quite a perceptive criticism of double standards (F90). What she fails to understand is that male honour insists that women should be virgins when they are brought to the marriage bed (this is to ensure that men do not marry into cuckoldry), yet *men* do not have to be virgins when they marry. After marriage society tolerates the infidelities of married women (provided there is a certain discretion maintained). Cécile naively thinks that her love for Danceny before her marriage to Gercourt ought logically to be as acceptable as a married woman's infidelity. Yet Cécile is the woman who later will have no qualms about posing as virtuous before her lover Danceny (L117), keeping him at arm's length, when she has just been "debauched" by Valmont.

Later on in the novel, Prévan is rehabilitated after his ostracism for what society, which now in turn ostracises Merteuil for her deceit, could only view at the time as attempted rape. This is hardly the triumph of virtue. [4] Prévan is no better than the woman who made him her victim. Without moral scruples, they both wanted to make a conquest simply in order to boast about it (of course Merteuil could only do this privately, and to Valmont). Society tolerates a double standard: men can sleep with whomever they wish—if the women are willing, that is—and vaunt their sexual prowess openly, for their reputations are thereby enhanced, but women must protect their virtue, or at least their public reputation for virtue, and this Mertueil has been unable to do. A society purely concerned with maintaining appearances is quite prepared to put up with sexual hypocrities who thrive on double standards, provided they are not unmasked. [5]

The second point (to which we will return) concerns the moralisers in the book.

In L.32, Mme de Volanges warns the Présidente against Valmont. In the opening paragraphs this letter shows a certain amount of good sense and penetration, and the simple point emerges that if Mme de Tourvel will not accept good advice, then she alone must be held responsible for the ultimate consequences. All the same we realise that Mme de Volanges is being manipulated by Mme de Merteuil, who wants to frustrate the developing relationship between the Présidente and Valmont. L.31 includes the tell-tale phrase about the "secrets" that Mme de Merteuil has to convey to Cécile's mother, and L.32 shows all the signs of being scripted by the Marquise. It is very likely that Merteuil has subtly played upon Mme de Volanges's guilt about her past to make sure that her warnings against Valmont are conveyed in the most effective way possible (compare her tactics in L.104, which are based on the knowledge 'que la bonne Dame a eu ses petites faiblesses comme une autre', F309). [6] L.32 is not objective disinterested advice; Mme de Volanges has herself acted imprudently 'dans son jeune temps' (F309), and her strident admonition conceals, or perhaps belatedly compensates for, her own past mistakes. [7] In any case, the final irony of the book (F473; see the end of this chapter) invalidates Mme de Volanges's credentials as a sustaining source of moral insight and advice. Similarly the moral usefulness of Mme de Rosemonde's correspondence with the Présidente is minimal (Rosemonde has a soft spot for her nephew: v. F327, F368)—in fact in small ways she unconsciously encourages her love (v. L.103, F295 & 296, and L.122, F350). It is by seeing the feet of clay of the moralisers in the book that the reader is led to question whether he is himself in the right position to make superficial moral judgements (such as those in the 'Préface du rédacteur'). 'He that is without sin among you, let him first cast a stone at her' (*John* , VIII, 7).

The third point concerns the varieties and degrees of hypocrisy in the book.

Les Liaisons is, in many ways, a chronicle of contemporary hypocrisy: let us give some examples. Danceny is double-faced in his dual affair, though he is not a deliberate hypocrite, for his feelings for Mme de Merteuil initially (L.116)—and, arguably, later (L.148)—involve unconscious self-deception: there is perhaps more naivety than conscious deceit in the man. As regards Cécile, Merteuil's penetrating analysis in L.105 (F303) uncovers the girl's lack of 'bonne foi'. We have to suppose that Cécile is aware of pretending to be virtuous before Danceny to preserve appearances when she has lost her virtue to Valmont—see L.117, dictated by the Vicomte; it is not certain, however, that she is mindful of the ironies he builds into this letter (a realisation which would strengthen her deception): 'Il fait tout comme vous feriez vous-même' (F341). Even the Présidente indulges in small duplicities amounting, at times, to hypocrisy, and caused by her growing but unacknowledged love. Valmont's savage attack on her hypocrisy in L.25 (F86) is grossly unfair in the wake of L.21 and coming from a man whose hypocritical role reversal involves his posing as the virtuous victim of a 'belle dame sans merci', while his assumption of her carefully planned deception in L.100 (F285-6)—a means of justifying his incredible blindness and misunderstanding of female psychology in L.99— is largely a projection of his own duplex tactics. Yet in L.11 Tourvel does, it is true, use the excuse that her husband will be surprised at her fickleness in leaving Rosemonde's château, to lend support to the unconscious reasons of her heart (she wants to avoid being separated from Valmont). In L.22 she describes the Vicomte's act of charity to Mme de Volanges, but suppresses the fact that she has had him tailed—indirect proof of her emotional interest in him. Taking fright at Valmont's threat to her virtue, she gets him to agree to go away. Yet her letters to Mme de Volanges insinuate that she is getting rid of him to please her "moral adviser", rather than out of the fear of any real danger. In L.45, F132, there is a touch of self-deception or hypocrisy in her feeling that she has cheated Mme de Rosemonde out of the company of her nephew simply for the sake of obeying Mme de Volanges. She is emotionally vulnerable to Valmont, but not prepared to admit it.

In the kingdom of involuntary hypocrites the conscious hypocrite reigns supreme. Illustrations of the Vicomte's skill in the genre can be found in L.44, F128 ('Je ne veux pas abuser de votre situation'—precisely what he is doing, though not sexually); in L.83, F233; in L.84, F237 ('Je hais tout ce qui a l'air de la tromperie'); and in L.96, F269—cp. F235. Valmont's hypocritical explanation of Emilie's laughter is something of a classic, too: compare L.137, F394 with L.138, F397. Of course Valmont is adept at posing as the virtuous romantic (L.68), or at donning the mask of virtue (L.120) whenever it suits his purposes as a seducer, and the juxtaposition of his letter to Anselme (L.120) with L.121—where Merteuil, posing as virtuous before Danceny, ends her letter to him thus: 'Sur ce, mon cher Chevalier, je prie Dieu qu'il vous ait en [sa] sainte et digne garde' (F349)— is clearly designed to make the reader aware that the chief protagonists are Tartuffes of comparable quality.

It is Mme de Merteuil who is the living embodiment of hypocrisy in the book, and L.104 is the most glaring instance of her exploitation of the gentle art. In L.104, the Marquise can pretend to argue out of the sense of propriety which she had shown in L.63 (v. F166) and in the totally hypocritical L.87. Alleging that she has the mother's best interests at heart she comes out in favour of Cécile's marriage with Gercourt and against Mme de Volanges's new plan that the girl should marry Danceny, her heart's desire, for whom Cécile is mistakenly assumed to be pining. We, the readers, know that she is really making sure that her revenge on Gercourt (Valmont's seduction of Cécile) will not be evaded. L.104 is seemingly moral advice for totally immoral purposes. While it is true that there are some fleeting similarities between the argument and language of L.81 and that of L.104 which might superficially seem to lessen the duplicity, [8] Merteuil's hypocritical deception is made even more striking to the reader by the juxtaposition of L.104 with the thoroughly immoral but impeccable logic of L.105, where the Marquise, advising Cécile to accept Valmont as a full-time lover, presents the advantages of hypocrisy to Cécile in a neat paradox: 'et pour avoir le double mérite, aux yeux de l'un de sacrifier l'amour, à ceux de l'autre, d'y résister, il ne vous en coûtera que d'en goûter les plaisirs' (F304). Reading in sequence and comparing Letters 104, 105 and 106 (the last-named with its revelations on F308-9) leaves the reader in no doubt as to Laclos's point: in a hypocritical society it is all too often only a question of appealing superficially to the "correct" sentiments, making the right moral noises, appearing virtuous.

Laclos's critical view of hypocrisy is complex. If society is based on façade, if women have a reputation for virtue purely for public consumption, and private lives of a very different calibre, then a woman who lives on her wits, and exposes that hypocrisy as she makes capital out of it, is unintentionally performing an important moral service. Indeed, it could be said she is merely using the weapons of her sex in an unequal struggle where men have unfair advantages. Yet, as the arch-exponent of hypocrisy, Mme de Merteuil must, at the end of the book, be exposed, in order to make a strong moral point. Since the immorality of her conduct precisely thrives upon her ability hypocritically to exploit a public reputation for virtue as a cover for vice, the disclosure of her hypocrisy through Danceny's making public L.81 (F456) means that everybody has now rumbled her system and her "principles". It is the ripping off of the mask of the hypocrite, [9] and this is made even more telling by the heavy irony that Merteuil is condemned as a result of writing L.81 (which is ultimately used as evidence against her) when in that very letter she advised against ever writing letters (F227)—an effective moral irony indeed.[10] *Les Liaisons* ends with none of her schemes intact and with her credibility totally destroyed. Moreover, society itself hardly has the moral authority to censure.[11] Ultimately we are left with the ironic awareness that society may sacrifice its scapegoats, but will no doubt go on actively tolerating a social system based on double standards for men and women (Prévan is socially acceptable but not Merteuil, though their sexual aims were the same), and on the impersonation not the practice of virtue. It may be a misjudgement to lament that Merteuil's ostracism by society in the final pages of the novel is simply a social punishment and therefore inadequate retribution for her immoral behaviour, for is it not an even more effective, profoundly moral irony that the hypocritical Merteuil should be condemned in the name of a notion of right and wrong to which only lip service is ever paid, and end up an outcast from a society which is itself hypocritical ? [12]

*****

The second area for discussion is that of the dénouement .

If the book had a sentimental morality, then Valmont's death in the duel ought to be the price he pays for abandoning the Présidente. One critic argues that perhaps Valmont does not defend himself properly in the fight with Danceny as a way of making reparation (in effect by suicide) for deserting the Présidente.[13] But nothing in the text indicates suicide. On the day, Valmont is the less incisive swordsman. In actual fact Valmont dies because of his involvement with Cécile: Danceny challenges him to the duel on discovering, through Merteuil, that Valmont had tricked him into unknowingly helping him to seduce Cécile.[14] Death is not an equitable punishment for Valmont's treatment of the naive and over-malleable Cécile, whereas it would be for his treachery towards such a paragon as Tourvel, who dies of love. It is the remarkable juxtaposition of the deaths of Valmont and the Présidente which encourages the belief that some kind of sentimental justice (self-inflicted by Valmont) is being meted out.

Another contentious issue, though possibly one of greater importance for the general exegesis of this novel, concerns *vraisemblance* and irony in the dénouement. In the 'Préface du rédacteur' the "editor" claimed 'c'est rendre un service aux mœurs que de dévoiler les moyens qu'emploient ceux qui en ont de mauvaises pour corrompre ceux qui en ont de bonnes' (F29). Yet is not the impression conveyed by *Les Liaisons* that these methods are intelligent, effective, ingenious, and based on a sound knowledge of psychology ? The argument would then run that the death of Valmont and the disgrace of Merteuil are artifically contrived to ensure that the wicked get their just deserts and are punished because convention demands it, but that Laclos's real sympathies are with his libertines who unleash their superior, malicious, manipulative intelligence to such effect upon their laughably naive victims, before being disposed of with deliberate improbability and undue haste—an ironic window-dressing of morality which is meant to deceive no-one.[15]

This interpretation is unreliable for several reasons. Firstly it does not make allowances for how far back the battle between Valmont and Merteuil goes—to L.113 and the Marquise's announcement of the man she has chosen as her new lover. The choice of Danceny gives her good grounds not to abide by the bargain of L.20, F70, now that its original purpose—the quick freeing of Valmont from Tourvel in order for him to seduce Cécile—no longer obtains, for the Vicomte can, so she has arranged it, run two affairs in tandem; L.20 proposes an agreement which, after the insulting L.125, she will have no intention of keeping, when a new lover is uppermost in her thoughts and when her revenge upon Gercourt seems assured. Indeed, a final clash between the two protagonists is the logical outcome of their rivalry and underhand manipulation of each other which the reader has witnessed throughout the book. [16] Moreover, it is because Valmont crucially departs from one of his libertine principles (namely that of avoiding emotional involvement with his victim) that he overvalues Mme de Tourvel, is manoeuvred by Merteuil into breaking with the Présidente to prove that he does not; and when Merteuil does not reciprocate by sacrificing Danceny (as she inevitably will not, on being faced with evidence of Valmont's continuing love) the clash intensifies. Heightened, embittered, ritualised rivalry is transformed into a personal duel (in which Danceny will, in effect, act as Merteuil's proxy duellist, avenging the insult of L.158) where the icy self-control which is supposed to distinguish the Marquise from ordinary mortals breaks down. The libertines destroy each other, therefore, and dispose of themselves, because, by a fatal flaw of intelligence, they lack the wit to live up to their own principles. [17] These supposedly incomparable intelligent beings are at the mercy of very human passions of pride and vanity which ultimately cause their downfall. Laclos establishes how effective they are in manipulating and corrupting those around them,

31

and how ineffective they are in handling themselves, when there is nobody left to corrupt and nothing on which to exercise their intelligence but themselves. Lacking the capacity for self-sacrificing love, two opposing "higher intelligences", motivated essentially by self-interest and self-image and unwilling to make concessions, must inevitably end up annihilating one another, after spreading deceit, corruption and death on all sides. [18]

Les Liaisons cannot be represented as a disguised apology for aristocratic libertinism with an unbelievable moral ending stuck on to placate the censors. There is no glorification of excessive sexual appetites. Libertinage is shown to be one of the fine arts like hunting or war. The carnality of the description of various sexual encounters is usually subordinated to the intellectual joys that Valmont and Merteuil find in precisely executed manoeuvres. The Vicomte and the Marquise revel not in mere sensual appetite but in the intellectual gratification of achieving difficult objectives. [19] As readers we become voyeuristic accomplices participating in the cerebral pleasures of these two self-spectators who enjoy the exercise of their power; fascinated by the skill, foresight, and calculation of effects involved, we may initially suspend moral judgement; but ultimately it is with ironic amusement that we note the intellectual and emotional bankruptcy of the two rivals who turn on each other at the end of the book. Is this not "conquer or perish" with a vengeance ? What alternatives are there to the present ending as we have it, given the *données* of the plot ? If Gercourt had been fortuitously killed off, say in a duel in Italy; if Danceny had left his order and married Cécile; if Père Anselme had reconciled a surviving Présidente with her husband, and if Valmont and Merteuil had re-established their old relationship, this would certainly be less credible than in the moral ending we do have, with its tragic, noble death of Tourvel, the shriven victim of the predatory male and of her own weakness, emotional myopia; with its chance of repentance for the less notable sinners; and with its punishment for the irredeemably wicked. This puts paid to the career of the Marquise but (in an ironic acknowledgment of male hegemony) allows the satanic Valmont to benefit from an heroic, virtuous death and a temporarily protected reputation.There is no "happily-ever-after" ending here to confound us with its inanity. For *Les Liaisons* is truly tragic: each human plan carries within it the fatal prognosis of failure or perversion; events of the dénouement unfold swiftly with the tragic inevitability of a classical French tragedy, [20] as the chief protagonists become locked in a doomed struggle which at times seems as mechanically predetermined as the mechanistic behaviour they had dismissed so penetratingly (F282, 308, 362), cogs in the *machine infernale* of Eros and hubris which they once so proudly controlled.

It is possible to distinguish between those aspects of the dénouement whose *raison d'être* stems from the plot and the natural run of events, and those whose *invraisemblance* can be accepted and seen as deliberately engineered in order to make a more subtle moral point. Valmont's death is not contrived; it is the logical culmination of his rivalry with the Marquise, and the duel is the inevitable result of Danceny's punctilious sense of honour (already demonstrated in L.66; and cf. L.169). Merteuil's social exposure and ostracism, which occur because one breach of confidentiality (L.162) inevitably leads to another (L.168), are the natural outcome of Valmont's desire for some revenge, even if only posthumous: an ironically fitting punishment for a hypocrite to become the ritual victim of a hypocritical society. Even if the loss of the court case by the Marquise, her sudden contraction of smallpox, and the positively medieval (but effective) moral judgement of her total disfigurement by the disease (see L.175, F472) seem capriciously accidental, because a final justice arrives providentially, is it any the less justice ? It is surely fitting that a "superior" intelligence such as she is should be let down by inferior intellects, for, when the bubble of her public reputation bursts, her lawyers fail to make capital out of the open prejudice no doubt shown to her (cp. F470)—the reader is, in any case, forewarned by L.134: 'Savez-vous que mon procès m'inquiète un peu ?' (F388). Fitting, too, that a woman who is conscious of growing old (L.121, F348-9) [21] and sufficiently obsessed with her appearance and beauty to want to attract Danceny away from Cécile, the woman he originally thought more beautiful than her (F62), should lose in this way (L.175), through a stroke of fate, her good looks and thus her power over men. Appropriately she who had seen herself as not, like Valmont, 'donnant tout au hasard' (F52), she who had determined to play God, foreseeing and controlling the destiny of lesser mortals (L.63), becomes subject to a blind Fate, lacking an eye just as she had lacked foresight of the outcome of the duel. [22]

Granted that this aspect of the ending (L.175) is *invraisemblable* , does this necessarily mean that Laclos really sympathises with Merteuil and wishes to be seen to be ironically sacrificing her to what he considers the boring old moral cliché that the wicked must pay for their misdeeds ? It seems more likely that Laclos is exploiting the improbability of this conjuncture of circumstances in order to hint, with the wry sardonic smile of the true satirist, that in real life (if not in the contrived endings of novels—by reading which society perhaps salves its guilty conscience) the real villains like Merteuil usually *do* avoid proper retribution, [23] just as less notorious offenders do not have to pay a penalty for their weakness. In the book Cécile and the Présidente both take refuge in a convent: one to seek repentance, the other to suffer an untimely death. In the hard-bitten society of the eighteenth century, this pathetic attempt to return to childhood innocence would no doubt be so uncharacteristic as to be laughed out of court as any kind of pragmatic solution to these women's problems—despite, that is, the prevailing vogue for sensibility. Here we are reminded of the savage moral irony that Laclos highlights at the end of the 'Avertissement de l'éditeur'

(F26). The very fact that the reader of those times, in collusion with the ironic "éditeur", can be assumed to regard as highly unlikely what happens to the Présidente and to Cécile—and, for the sake of argument, could we not include in the category of improbable events the fate of *Merteuil* in L.175 ?—involves a telling criticism of contemporary mores (v . *supra,* page 21).

Laclos's "real sympathies" are not easy to determine. How menacing Merteuil and Valmont appear to us is surely a measure of his creative empathy with his characters. But he sides with them, making them credible and powerful figures, particularly because he needs them to make a rather un-Rousseauesque point. This point he underlines by presenting a strong contrast between the Présidente on the one hand, and, on the other, the Vicomte and the Marquise who are never willing to be duped by sentiment. Valmont seems aware of the necessity to re-establish self-mastery whenever his feelings run away with him (L.125), and indeed, however much he may later regret it, he ruthlessly jettisons Mme de Tourvel as much to prove to himself that he is not 'maîtrisé comme un écolier, par un sentiment involontaire et inconnu' (F358) as to try to show affection for Merteuil (F406). The Marquise explains in L.81 how she herself achieved self-mastery as a young woman, distinguishing herself from those 'femmes à délire, et qui se disent à *sentiments* ' (like Cécile—at that stage, F221, before L.105) and also from those 'femmes actives dans leur oisiveté, que vous nommez *sensibles* ' (F222—like the Présidente): two types whose delusions and weaknesses she stigmatizes. For she has come to the conclusion that 'l'amour, que l'on nous vante comme la cause de nos plaisirs, n'en est plus que le prétexte' (F225). By contrast, Mme de Tourvel, though 'an intelligent woman endowed with principle and character [...] is [...] as defenceless as Cécile against treachery, because she allows herself to be guided by her feelings, and indeed has no other standard for distinguishing the true from the false .' [24] Laclos, by inducing us to side with Valmont and Merteuil, Mead says, makes us 'witnesses not to a mere seduction but to what might be called the *assassination of sensibility* and its claims to "usefulness" as a way of life', [25] after the moral basis of the Présidente's potential appeal to our sympathy as the victim of Valmont has been weakened by her hypocrisy in L.45, by her partial awareness of her own responsibility (e.g. L.67, F179), and by her being partly conscious of her own blindness. [26] The moral is that virtue is no protection against vice and an unscrupulous intelligence for a woman who is the prey of her feelings and whose sense of reality is distorted by emotion. But the ironic message of the dénouement is that those masters and manipulators of sentiment, Valmont and Merteuil, are finally undone by their inability to master common human feelings of hurt pride and vanity which turn their rivalry into a battle for superiority where neither side will win.

Reflecting on this parable about control and self-control we may initially feel, as Cherpack does, that the novel portrays the 'baneful effects of passion.' Cécile and Danceny dramatise the effects of passion on the ignorant and inexperienced in an inconsistent society. The Présidente shows the feebleness of conventional virtue when confronted by passion. Even the intelligence of Valmont and Merteuil is ultimately defeated by passion as their final passionate battle for mastery of each other bears out. [27]

Next we may ask ourselves: are the Vicomte and the Marquise brought down by a failure to control love, or by a failure to love, simply ? Had Valmont rated his image as a careless and unfeeling rake as less important than his love for the Présidente he would not have sent her the fatal letter (see L.142), and thus not have insisted on an equivalent sacrifice from Merteuil (F427-8); nor, when Tourvel finally slipped from his grasp (L.154), manoeuvred to get it in such an insulting way (L.155, L.158). Surrendering to his feelings for the

Présidente, he could have put out of his mind the bargain of L.20 and broken off the correspondence with Merteuil. Had the Marquise been truly in love with Valmont—not merely nostalgic in a *calculating* way about their former affair in order to win "sacrifices" from him that she had no intention of reciprocating (L.131, end)—she would have taken the hint of L.142 'amour [...] pour qui ?' (F406) and chosen to regard Valmont's sacrifice of Tourvel as proof of his love for her, Merteuil; and she would not have been so insistent on continuing the game of one-upmanship to the bitter end (see L.162 and her counterstroke to L.158). For although Merteuil presumably did not know that Mme de Tourvel was terminally ill, or that Valmont's last-minute attempt to recall her to life had been frustrated (L.154), she was convinced that the Vicomte could never countermand the lethal break-off letter (see L.145, F412). She could therefore have chosen to see L.158 not as an intolerable humiliation, but as Valmont's brutal method of attempting to drive a wedge between herself and Danceny so that the two former lovers could come together again with a balance of salvaged pride, for each would have forced the other to give up his preferred partner. At specific points, then, the two libertines could be saved from a fight to the finish by self-sacrificing love which rejects *amour-propre* as it accepts the dissolution of the fatal twin triangle of relationships in which they are trapped. In the event, overbearing intelligence, while blind to the danger of self-love, regards emotional involvement as a humiliating weakness; therefore in the final analysis "pusillanimous" feelings (on both sides ?) are sacrificed to vanity and self-image masquerading as rational control and calculation. *Les Liaisons* , in fine, does have a sentimental message at least in so far as it implicitly argues against the self-centred suppression of genuine feeling as strongly as it does against the dangers of a blinkered emotionalism.

The higher the pretensions of Valmont and Merteuil, the more critical are the flaws in their psychological make-up and the greater their resulting fall. Laclos is not asking us as readers to conclude from the turn of events that we should model ourselves upon his satanic characters but eschew their vanity and inconsistency. [28] Is it possible to be as satanic as they are even *with* their human weaknesses? *Les Liaisons* , we feel at times, demonstrates pure evil at work in the world. Maliciousness and wrong-doing seem gratuitous. There is no proportion between the harm those who become their victims have supposedly done Merteuil and Valmont and the terrible revenge they exercise upon them. [29] The Présidente, for instance, must pay the penalty simply for representing an alternative morality of chastity and devout virtue (F335); a few pages of ineffective advice from Mme de Volanges to the Présidente means that Valmont will ruin her daughter; a whole Machiavellian edifice of planning and manipulation by the Marquise is brought to bear on the pale insignificant figure of Gercourt, who just happens to be an ex-lover of hers who has left her but not by her arrangement or with her consent (v. F36, and cp. F220-221). The Vicomte and Merteuil carelessly play with their victims like children pulling the wings off butterflies. There is a fundamental perversity about behaving badly purely for the sake of behaving badly. [30] Pure evil seems triumphant, for among the other characters of the book there is no representative of pure virtue, tested in action, to oppose it. Evil can only be destroyed from within, by a vice: self-love. But, curiously enough, virtue, in the least expected place, perhaps has its part to play, too. By an ironic paradox, it may be partly because they still possess a rudimentary moral sense of justice that Merteuil and Valmont's metaphorical fencing with words becomes a literal duel where no compromise is possible. In L.151 the Vicomte is appalled at the injustice of Merteuil's not responding to his sacrifice of Tourvel for her by her relinquishing Danceny for him; the end of L.152, while using the sensibility argument polemically to justify denying Valmont his reward, embodies the Marquise's notion of fairness. Ironically the two arch-immoralists apply normal standards of justice perhaps for the first time in their lives, taking their quarrel to the point of no return, which means that their own immoral standards and principles inevitably must perish along with them. Even apparently pure evil is not completely pure, for it has some redeeming but insidious human defects which contribute to its destruction. The dangers of pure unalloyed depravity and what it is capable of when unchecked thereby emerge even more starkly as a salutary warning. [31]

As the tragic dénouement illustrates, events in themselves have an implicit morality, even if, by the laws of the letter-novel genre, it is the reader who must accurately assess their validity and draw his own conclusions. In the absence of a single overall narrator, broadly evaluating the actions of his characters (not fabricating banal editorial footnotes, e.g. F51), Laclos leaves it to the moralisers among the letter writers to rustle their petticoats indignantly and mouth the proper sentiments as they try to draw the lesson from experience at the end of the book. Typically he undercuts their spurious didacticism with irony which makes the reader look over his own shoulder, for it points to the hazards of drawing moral conclusions without forethought.

Ironically, Mme de Rosemonde mouths platitudes about '[les] bornes prescrites par les Lois et la Religion' and lectures Danceny (L.171) on his moral responsibility when her reliability as a mentor is at its lowest ebb. For, having, despite her pious presentation, exacerbated Mme de Tourvel's love (F350), she has kept her greatest reservations on Valmont's character and the considerable danger the Présidente has been exposed to, and, she thinks, escaped from, till her *fifth* letter (L.126) *when it is too late* (an irony, incidentally, which mocks not moral advice as such, but ineffective misplaced advice, Rosemonde's rheumaticky arm notwithstanding). [32] Yet this is the women who now, despite nebulous references to Valmont's 'torts'

(F464), in effect whitewashes her nephew and pins the blame for Cécile's corruption squarely on the ineffectual lover Danceny: 'celui qui le premier tente de séduire un cœur encore honnête et simple se rend par là même le premier fauteur de sa corruption, et doit être à jamais comptable des excès et des égarements qui la suivent' (L.171, F465). This is the woman who is in possession of correspondence (F459) which proves that her dear nephew's and Merteuil's concerted effort to have the unenterprising Danceny seduce Cécile was so fruitless that Valmont himself was able to step into Danceny's shoes to do the job for him. Admittedly Mme de Rosemonde's main motivation in this paragraph in L.171 is morally to browbeat Danceny and get him to hand over Cécile's letters, but how truly Danceny must appreciate her attribution of blame when they have both read Valmont's account of his corruption of Cécile, L.96 (which led to the duel)! Had he been privy to *Rosemonde* 's correspondence, too, and less shamefaced about his double affair, he might well have felt like throwing back in her teeth 'l'amour est un sentiment indépendant, que la prudence peut faire éviter, mais qu'elle ne saurait vaincre' (L.126, F368). But of course if family honour requires the dispensing of hypocrisies, then so be it... [33]

Mme de Volanges's end comments are a model not of hypocrisy but of sheer ineptitude and blindness. Referring to the deaths of Valmont and of his victim Tourvel and to the disgrace of Merteuil, in L.173 she opines: 'Je vois bien dans tout cela les méchants punis; mais je n'y trouve nulle consolation pour leurs malheureuses victimes' (F470). Yet is not the Présidente the prey of her own emotionalism, granted, but no less a martyr to Mme de Volanges's conventionality (see L.154) ? It is of course those with the most to hide (F309) who take the strictest moral line. If the choice was between saving Mme de Tourvel's life by condoning adultery, or letting her die, then there can be no doubt which would be the better course of action, morally speaking.

A final irony exposes Mme de Volanges's limited moral vision. At the end of the book she exclaims:

> Qui pourrait ne pas frémir en songeant aux malheurs que peut causer une seule liaison dangereuse! et quelles peines ne s'éviterait-on point en y réfléchissant davantage! Quelle femme ne fuirait pas au premier propos d'un séducteur? Quelle mère pourrait, sans trembler, voir une autre personne qu'elle parler à sa fille ? Mais ces réflexions tardives n'arrivent jamais qu'après l'événement...(L.175, F473).

The irony is that the Présidente was very aware at various points along the path to her seduction of what sacrifices her virtue was making to her love (v. L.124, F354-5) and the suffering and misery it was causing her (v. L.90). Mme de Volanges thinks, too, that she is adducing the bitter lesson from experience (her daughter's affair with Danceny), but ironically she is not even "wise after the event", for she knows nothing of Cécile's corruption by Valmont (see L.173). She knows no more about Cécile's miscarriage than she did about her seduction (cp. L.98). Remarks made as if consciously beating her breast and expiating her guilt are really an unconscious condemnation of her behaviour. In one sense what she says is much truer than she realises. She thinks she can see the mote in the eye of her dead sister Tourvel ('Qui pourrait ne pas frémir en songeant aux malheurs que peut causer une seule liaison dangereuse' is a rather self-righteous repetition of L.32, F97; compare F452), but she fails to see the beam in her own eye (*Matthew* , VII, 3).

This final irony makes us reflect on our own attitude to the book's moral message, and refers us back full circle to the 'Préface du rédacteur' with which we began and to remarks which, like those of Mme de Volanges, are equally equivocal because of the presence of irony. As attentive readers we will have noticed the *conscious* hypocrisy of a moral point similar to Mme de Volanges's made by the Marquise when she was posing as virtuous before Danceny in L.121:

> Mais pour peu qu'une femme raisonne, elle doit savoir
> qu'indépendamment de la faute qu'elle commet, une
> faiblesse est pour elle le plus grand des malheurs; et je ne
> conçois pas qu'aucune s'y laisse jamais prendre, quand
> elle peut avoir un moment pour y réfléchir. (F349)

'By painting such a picture of hypocrisy and self-righteous moralism in Mme de Volanges, who has the last word, and in the society for which she speaks, Laclos may renew our allegiance to the amoral intelligence of Valmont and the Marquise. Their egotistical manipulation of others seems the only adequate response to the bad faith of their contemporaries', says Peter Brooks, [34] perhaps forgetting that true hypocrisy is practically always conscious (here Mme de Volanges, whom the hypocritical Mme de Rosemonde has refused to enlighten, is simply blind), and that *Les Liaisons dangereuses* shows how the 'amoral intelligence' of Valmont and Merteuil fails, for pride or passion is destructive and there are no exceptions to this rule. Through Mme de Volanges's blindness at the end Laclos seems to be warning the reader against identifying a moral in the book but failing to see its application to his own life. True moralists are self-aware, and *intentionally* their own best critics; unfortunately Volanges, in the final sentences of the book, is no such thing—nor is any other blinkered *bien-pensant* to whose moral righteousness Laclos, through the "editor", satirically addresses himself in the 'Préface du rédacteur'. It is perfectly natural that the representatives of a society shocked to the core by the revelation of Merteuil's cynical exploitation of the gap between reality and appearance should revert to old habits of only seeing the surface of things and suffer from a kind of moral tunnel vision, but the reader who has lifted the mask cannot afford to be as complacent as they are.

*****

The 'Préface du rédacteur' and the 'Avertissement de l'éditeur' are not, morally speaking, irreconcilable as they are sometimes made out to be, nor is the presence of irony in the 'Préface' incompatible with the thesis that *Les Liaisons* does indeed have serious moral content; what this "deeper moral" consists of, it has been the purpose of this chapter to define, illustrate and interpret.

The dénouement is by no means improbable in every aspect; it should not be understood as ironically artificial in an amoral way, and the irony of fate and dramatic irony evident in the ending is the invention of a "moraliste" with an eye for human weakness, inconsistency and blindness, and their own appropriate punishments. As for the moralisers at the end, Mme de Rosemonde, though a sympathetic and stylish commentator, is not an innocent by-stander whose ex cathedra statements can always be respected; she is not necessarily the reliable "moral-message-bearer" she is sometimes taken for—any more than is Mme de Volanges. For depending upon the sophistication of the reader whom Laclos has in mind, the 'Préface' and the end of the book can be seen to offer either a "correct" moral viewpoint which it would be churlish to fault, or a satirical indictment of the complacent or bogus moralising of a superficial society, one of whose members is the "rédacteur" himself. [35]

Irony

> The more time you spend with a subject the less sure you
> are of where it begins and where it finishes.
>
> D.J. Enright, *The Alluring Problem: An Essay on Irony*

Let us begin by defining three types of irony.[1] Following Samuel
Johnson's definition, simple irony is the conveying of a meaning (often
satirical) by words whose literal meaning is the opposite; another term
for this is antiphrasis, and a good example occurs in the 'Avertissement
de l'éditeur' where we read:

> plusieurs des personnages que [l'Auteur] met en scène ont
> de si mauvaises mœurs, qu'il est impossible de supposer
> qu'ils   aient vécu dans notre siècle; dans ce siècle de
> philosophie, où   les lumières, répandues de toutes parts,
> ont rendu, comme   chacun sait, tous les hommes si
> honnêtes et toutes les femmes   si modestes et si réservées.
> (F25)

Secondly, in the figurative sense, the word "irony" can be applied
to 'a condition of affairs or events of a character opposite to what was,
or might naturally be, expected; a contradictory outcome of events as if
in mockery of the promise and fitness of things' (O.E.D.). This can be
tragic irony: if you like, 'the contrast between man with his hopes,
fears, wishes and undertakings, and a dark inflexible fate' (*ibid* ., e.g.
quoted).

Thirdly there is dramatic irony. This, Eric Partridge says, consists in
words plus situation, and occurs 'when the audience in a theatre, or the
reader of a book, perceives a crux, a significance, a point, that the
characters concerned do not perceive' (*Usage and abusage* , sub
'irony').

44

Wayne Booth asserts that:

> Whenever an author conveys to his reader an unspoken point, he creates a sense of collusion against all those, whether in the story or out of it, who do not get that point. Irony is always thus in part a device for excluding as well as for including, and those who are included, those who happen to have the necessary information to grasp the irony, cannot but derive at least part of their pleasure from a sense that others are excluded. In the irony with which we are concerned, the speaker is himself the butt of the ironic point. The author and his reader are secretly in collusion, behind the speaker's back, agreeing upon the standard by which he is found wanting.[2]

Dramatic irony is the most conspicuous form of irony in *Les Liaisons dangereuses* . The book's plot is based on the duplicity, deception and covert manipulation of Merteuil and Valmont; those letter writers ironically unaware of the character and ploys of these two are those who become their victims. The spectacle of the blindness, ignorance, shortsightedness or lack of circumspection of these victims, and of those on the sidelines too, is always likely to provoke the reader's amusement and scorn more than his pity. Certainly we have nothing but amused scorn for those individuals who moralise at the end of the book. Mme de Rosemonde and Mme de Volanges are blind in their pseudo-lucidity, for events of which they are blithely unaware ironically bear out their perception of moral danger (v. *supra* L.126 and L.175, discussed at the end of the last chapter). It is very probably the high proportion of dramatic ironies involving characters deceived by the libertines (to be illustrated later) which helps create the false impression in some critics' minds that Laclos's "real sympathies" lie with Merteuil and Valmont, and that therefore the dénouement and its ethical point are transparently bogus. Moreover the two main characters exploit a strain of cynical moralising, [3] an ironic dressing-up of immoral purposes in moral language, [4] an ironic identification with conventional viewpoints, [5] often so effectively as to make us, the readers, laugh aloud in complicity. It is all too easy to forget that some of the most piquant of all the ironies in the novel apply to the Vicomte and to the Marquise, who ultimately fail to square theory with practice, or are unaware of the implications of their words for themselves: [6] the reader is never in any doubt as to the "standard by which [they are] found wanting", for so often it is the standard which they have set for themselves.

*****

To start with, let us examine simple irony.

Since the values of the libertines subvert normal values, the Marquise and the Vicomte adopt a kind of "double-speak" where words ironically suggest the exact opposite of their normal, "honest" meanings. Thus Valmont can describe his dissolute life with Cécile in these terms: 'nous menions, votre Pupille et moi, une vie commode et réglée' (L.140, F400).

> In *Les Liaisons dangereuses* [...] words and notions are emptied of their meaning, turned inside out and upside down. Thus when Mme de Merteuil writes to Valmont about Cécile: '...si une fois vous formez cette petite...' or about Mme de Tourvel: 'peut-être si vous eussiez connu cette femme plus tôt en eussiez-vous pu faire quelque chose', she means exactly the opposite: *former* becomes *déformer* ; *faire* , *défaire* . (C.J. Greshoff, *art . cit* ., p. 396) [7]

Sometimes this language is coloured with medical metaphor: Merteuil's advice to Valmont on his corruption of Cécile is to 'forcer les *doses* ' (L.106, F307); 'elle a une sotte ingénuité qui n'a pas cédé même au *spécifique* que vous avez employé' (*id* ., F308, my italics in both cases).

The presence of a certain kind of metaphoric language is often an indicator of irony.

(i) There are stories with a sustained ironic presentation. For instance the ironic devices of L.85, Merteuil's account of her seduction of Prévan, rely on military metaphors ('sous ce drapeau banal', F239) and on classical reference ('le Cerbère', F245), as well as straightforward antiphrasis ('D'abord, son Domestique était sûr comme lui-même: en cela il ne trompait guère, l'un l'était bien autant que l'autre', F244; 'ils s'indignaient qu'on eût osé manquer *à leur vertueuse Maîtresse* ', F247, Merteuil's italics). More usually, ironic language crops up sporadically.

(ii) Military terms are found here and there, linked with notions of medieval chivalry, but used ironically as a kind of cynical corruption of the chivalric ideal. [8] In L.2 the Marquise, who wants Valmont to seduce Cécile, says:

> Je veux donc bien vous instruire de mes projets: mais jurez-moi qu'en fidèle Chevalier vous ne courrez aucune aventure que vous n'ayez mis celle-ci à fin. (F36)

He will have to demonstrate his fidelity to the Marquise by being unfaithful to her with another woman! Similarly in L.20 Mme de Merteuil, talking of Valmont's seduction of the Présidente and the letter proof of this, says:

> Venez donc, venez au plus tôt m'apporter le gage de votre triomphe: semblable à nos preux Chevaliers qui venaient déposer aux pieds de leurs Dames les fruits brillants de leur victoire. (F71)

Or again, in L.66 Valmont, mentioning in rather imaginative terms Danceny's reaction to the obstacles Merteuil has put in the way of his love for Cécile (see L.63, F167), declares:

> Danceny est tout de feu; et sûrement à la première occasion, vous n'aurez plus de reproches à lui faire. (F177)

So Danceny is to be a kind of "chevalier sans peur et sans reproche", like Bayard, but it is a strange proof of his courage that he will supposedly be able to perform the doughty feat of seducing the naive and willing Cécile: the chivalric-sounding tag "[sans] reproche" translates ironically as "capable of seducing Cécile". [9]

(iii) In tandem with this ironic chivalric terminology we note the ironic or semi-ironic use of religious language and comparisons. There are plenty of examples: L.4, F39—'nous prêchons la foi chacun de notre côté...; *id* ., F41—Mme de Rosemonde has no suspicion of the nature of the 'Divinité' that Valmont goes to worship at mass (i.e. the Présidente); L.10, F56— 'c'est au Sacrificateur à disposer du Temple'; L.63, F169—the comparison between Cécile and Mary Magdalene; L.81, F221—'vraies superstitieuses, (ces femmes [...] *à sentiments*) ont pour le Prêtre, le respect et la foi qui n'est dû qu'à la Divinité.' Perhaps the best example of a genuinely comic irony using religious language is to be found in L.110—and it is one which illustrates Malcolm Muggeridge's assertion that good taste and humour are a contradiction in terms, 'like a chaste whore'. [10] There (F320), Valmont likens Cécile's deferential treatment of him, leading to a renewal of their sexual acquaintance (as a result of L.105), to the conduct of a penitent towards her father confessor:

> Enfin, ce n'est que Samedi qu'on est venu tourner autour de moi et me balbutier quelques mots; encore prononcés si bas et tellement étouffés par la honte, qu'il était impossible de les entendre. Mais la rougeur qu'ils causèrent m'en fit deviner le sens. Jusque-la, je m'étais tenu fier: mais fléchi par un si plaisant repentir, je voulus bien promettre d'aller trouver le soir même la jolie Pénitente; et cette grâce de ma part, fut reçue avec toute la reconnaissance due à un si grand bienfait.

Cécile is expiating her "sin" of locking the door on Valmont (to use the latter's terminology) by sinning some more (in conventional terms). As we might expect from an author much given to symmetrical patterning of his work (v. *infra* , my chapter on 'Structure', *passim*) there is an obvious parallel to be found in the Valmont-Présidente affair. At the end of L.138 Valmont describes how he will try to make up with Mme de Tourvel after his (in fact, second) infidelity with Emilie:

> dans un moment, j'irai moi-même faire signer mon pardon: car dans les torts de cette espèce, il n'y a qu'une seule formule qui porte absolution générale, et celle-là ne s'expédie qu'en présence. (F398)

Simple irony is easy enough to pick out by reason of a certain exaggeration, preciosity, or rhetorical colouring which draws attention to itself. By contrast, *private* irony, done essentially for a character's own amusement, and not, as with most of the aforementioned examples and with some transparent syllepses such as L.48 and L.120, for the entertainment of an accomplice, is more difficult but more rewarding in the detection.[11] Let us illustrate this by referring to the end of L.121. Mme de Merteuil writes to Danceny:

> ce que je trouverais impardonnable à toute autre qu'à un enfant comme la petite Volanges, serait de ne pas savoir fuir un danger, dont elle a été suffisamment avertie par l'aveu qu'elle a fait de son amour. Vous autres hommes, vous n'avez pas d'idées de ce qu'est la vertu, et de ce qu'il en coûte pour la sacrifier! Mais pour qu'une femme raisonne, elle doit savoir qu'indépendamment de la faute qu'elle commet, une faiblesse est pour elle le plus grand des malheurs; et je ne conçois pas qu'aucune s'y laisse jamais prendre, quand elle peut avoir un moment pour y réfléchir.
> N'allez pas combattre cette idée, car c'est elle qui m'attache principalement à vous. Vous me sauverez des dangers de l'amour. (F349)

Mme de Merteuil is posturing as virtuous before Danceny in order to make him delicate and discreet in his pursuit of her. As part of her pretence to virtue she employs what could perhaps be seen as a coded reference to the Présidente, a forecast of what will happen to the Présidente in her affair with Valmont (based on predictions in L.115), as a means of paying court to Danceny. She suggests that she, Merteuil, is attached to him because she knows she will never show weakness with him (as Cécile has done, and as Tourvel will do with Valmont). Ironically she is actually inveigling Danceny into a non-virtuous relationship by standing on her virtue (cf. L.157, F439-40). 'Vous me sauverez des dangers de l'amour,' she says (F349), but rather than highlighting Danceny's honourable intentions she may, by a private irony, be implying either that he lacks the guts to make love to her, or that sexual indulgence with him will save her from the folly of emotional commitment (see L.81, F221). [12]

There are very many striking *ironies of plot* . Mme de Volanges's conviction that Valmont is scheming actually leads him into the schemes of L.21 (see F51-2; F58-9; F63-4). [13] Ironically it is Valmont's discovery of letters which to the discerning reader bear signs of Merteuil's treachery against him (L.32) that causes the Vicomte to desire not revenge on Merteuil, but the same revenge as Merteuil (see L.44, F130). When Mme de Volanges is apprised of her daughter's affair with Danceny it is a nice touch that she should try to protect her by taking her to the very château where Valmont will be at liberty to seduce her. Cécile is, in due course, seduced yet remains at the château, whereas the Présidente flees from it though her virtue is still intact. It is paradoxically anger at Valmont's feigned concern over her possible inability to handle Prévan which elicits Merteuil's explanations, in L.81, of her icy self-control. Valmont spends a great deal of time and energy writing letters to Tourvel in which he is merely mimicking the voice of true passion, then ends up really falling in love with her against his every principle (v. L.100, F286-7). Lloyd Free speaks of:

the ironic emotional converging of the psyches of two people who have antithetical moral positions. Madame de Tourvel believes she is morally immune to temptation and will convert Valmont, the notorious rake, to righteousness. Valmont operates on a similar premise, namely, that owing to his vast experience as a rake, he is immune to emotion and will seduce Madame de Tourvel to add new luster to his wordly reputation. As the novel progresses, each character, like those in Marivaux's plays, denies what is apparent—that they are falling in love. Indeed the irony of the Valmont and Tourvel subplot is that the two characters are unfaithful to their moral principles because each falls victim to love. (*art . cit* ., p. 38)

It is because of a virtue (the wish to humiliate her pride) that Tourvel loses her virtue (see L.124, F355). One of the arguments the Marquise uses to reject the possibility that she and Valmont might renew their old relationship for longer than just one night is that like two cardsharpers they will deceive each other (L.131). In the event they do deceive each other (L.155; L.162) even though they are not yet lovers once again. The Présidente dies ultimately as a result of receiving a letter of rejection (L.141) actually not composed by Valmont at all. Valmont, for his part, thinks he is ironically overstating the case when he talks, in L.144, of trying to find out 'si la sensible personne était morte ou mourante' (F408) on receiving the "fateful" letter, when, in reality, and by a greater irony, he is foretelling what will happen. The immediate cause of Mme de Tourvel's death is the news that Valmont has been killed in a duel—which we, the readers, know resulted from his affair with an entirely different woman (Cécile). The Vicomte uses the unreal threat of suicide as a lever in his seduction of Tourvel (v. L.58, L.125), yet according to some critics actually commits suicide for having abandoned her:

> Valmont, qui meurt pour son amante, la rejoint au tombeau; la mort scelle l'unité du couple et consacre la vérité du sentiment. Ironie suprême, une histoire vouée à la perversion se termine sur un triomphe de la nature et de

l'amour.[14]

Moreover he exploits the disclosure of private correspondence with Merteuil which will cause Prévan to be rehabilitated socially, so as to prove that men can never be beaten in the war of the sexes, yet himself dies the victim of a woman's pride. One of the people most affected by the Présidente's death—Mme de Rosemonde (v. F449-50)—is the woman who has indirectly by her letters helped Valmont seduce her (L.115, F335); made her surrender psychologically more probable,[15] nurturing Tourvel's love while ostensibly urging her to control it (L.122, F350); and warned her of the Vicomte's tendency to '[mettre] presque un prix égal à séduire [les femmes] et à les perdre' (L.126 F368) when this has already happened. For her part, the Marquise, commenting on Prévan's fate in L.85, says 'peut-être même ne se relèvera-t-il jamais du coup que je lui ai porté' (F238), but the 'peut-être', intended as understatement, turns out to be a very necessary qualification. Ironic understatement makes Merteuil's threat to expose Valmont and force him to leave the country a very real one (L.152), but the exile with which she threatens him is the exile she is forced into herself (L.175), largely as a result of the public disclosure (L.168) of a letter in which she advised against ever writing letters and thus leaving incriminating evidence (L.81). Valmont and Merteuil, those masters of self-control, are brought down in the end by uncontrolled pride and vanity; arch-immoralists and superhuman creations, they yet retain a rudimentary sense of justice and exhibit human weaknesses by which they are finally undone (see the previous chapter).[16]

*****

Let us now consider dramatic irony, as far as it applies to the chief protagonists' victims.

In L.11, unaware of Valmont's plans to seduce her or of the Marquise's true character, the Présidente thinks that the proof that Valmont is not at heart a libertine is the fact that he is a devoted friend of the 'estimable' Mme de Merteuil (F58). The highly moral Mme de Tourvel, proving her virtue by detecting virtue in others (where it does not exist), calls Valmont's payment of the poor peasant family's taxes a 'vertueuse action' (L.22, F77). We know from L.21 that it is merely a pretence of virtue on Valmont's part in order to win over the woman whom he is pursuing, and that he regards it as no more significant than the payment one would make to a prostitute:

> l'ayant, en quelque sorte, ainsi payée d'avance, j'aurai le droit d'en disposer à ma fantaisie, sans avoir de reproche à me faire. (F75)

The Présidente even detects that this is *planned* charity: what ought to have alerted her suspicion of an act done for effect is simply confirmation of Valmont's genuine virtue in her eyes, for as she says:

> ce n'est même plus seulement une compassion passagère, et que l'occasion détermine; c'est le projet formé de faire du bien; c'est la sollicitude de la bienfaisance; c'est la plus belle vertu des plus belles âmes. (L.22, F77)

Later the Présidente, who can be very clear-sighted at times (L.50, F141), probably thinks that Valmont's ill-health (the result of sexual indulgence with Cécile) is a sign of his unrequited love (L.110; L.114). At a time when the Vicomte is preparing to come and seduce her, she thinks he is coming to see her to 'me dire lui-même que je ne lui suis plus rien, que l'impression faible et passagère que j'avais faite sur lui est entièrement effacée' (F355). Equally striking is the ironic clash between Tourvel's expectations of Valmont's cold indifference towards her in the meeting he has got Anselme to arrange, and Valmont's virtuoso performance during the actual seduction scene where he pulls out all the emotional stops (L.125, F361 and F363).

Dramatic irony always involves, is always based on, a contrast between the reader's privileged knowledge of the truth and of real motivation, and the misapprehensions, ignorance, or wilful blindness of the character who is the butt of the irony. The Présidente is not naturally ingenuous; love is blind and love has made her blind. This contrast is perhaps at its sharpest where the most naturally naive of the characters in the book are those concerned.

Take Cécile, for instance. Cécile ludicrously thinks she is being perceptive in detecting Merteuil's doubts about any future married happiness for the girl with Gercourt (L.39, F114), when in fact the Marquise has deliberately fostered this impression to ensure that Cécile makes amorous hay while the sun shines (see L.38, F113-4). When her affair with Danceny is discovered, Cécile's doubts about her maid Joséphine, and her faith in Merteuil (L.61, F163), are ironically misplaced in the context of L.63, F165-6. Again the reader is perfectly aware that thanks to Mme de Merteuil's machinations (L.63) Valmont is able to return to the château bent on pursuing his seduction of the Présidente, and (so the initial plan goes) on inducing Danceny to seduce Cécile so that he, Valmont, will get his own back on Mme de Volanges through damaging her daughter (L.44). Yet in L.75 Cécile, who has been invited there too, surmises:

> J'ai peur que [Valmont] ne s'ennuie bientôt de la vie qu'on mène ici, et qu'il ne s'en retourne à Paris; cela serait bien fâcheux. Il faut qu'il ait bien bon cœur d'être venu exprès pour rendre service à son ami [Danceny] et à moi! (F196)

But of course Valmont is obsessed with the Présidente, and is not acting as a go-between for Cécile and Danceny out of the kindness of his heart...[17]

Mme de Volanges is another naturally naive character who becomes the target of irony. In L.9, when she warns the Présidente against Valmont, one of her arguments is this:

de toutes les femmes auxquelles il a rendu des soins, succès ou non, il n'en est point qui n'aient eu à s'en plaindre. La seule Marquise de Merteuil fait l'exception à cette règle générale; seule, elle a su lui résister et enchaîner sa méchanceté. J'avoue que ce trait de sa vie est celui qui lui fait le plus d'honneur à mes yeux: aussi a-t-il suffi pour la justifier pleinement aux yeux de tous de quelques inconséquences qu'on avait à lui reprocher dans le début de son veuvage. (F51)

It is ironic, not to say hypocritical, that Mme de Volanges should mention in a mealy-mouthed, rather moralistic way the Marquise's indiscretions, when she has been guilty of indiscretions herself in her flighty youth (v. L.106, F309); ironic that she should think that Merteuil's indiscretions were a sign of weakness rather than strength (see L.81, F226); ironic, finally, that she should so completely misunderstand the nature of the Valmont-Merteuil relationship. Naturally enough, later on, the person to whom she chooses to confide her worries about her daughter (in L.98) is the least trustworthy she could possibly have picked—Mme de Merteuil. Also, to think that she could have mistaken Cécile's ravaged look after her first night with Valmont for a romantic yearning for Danceny, brings a wry smile to the lips of any reader: an irony to savour. 'Heureusement'—she says, when what she means, if she only knew it, is 'malheureusement'—'j'ai eu la prudence [read 'imprudence'] de ne lui faire aucune question, et elle n'a pas osé m'en dire davantage: mais il n'en est pas moins clair que c'est cette malheureuse passion [for Danceny!] qui la tourmente' (L.98, F276: it is *not* clear—this is a completely false assumption). Mme de Volanges even thinks that she is making Cécile pay for her constancy to Danceny, at the very point at which Cécile has been forced to be unfaithful to him! (*ibid*.) L.104, Merteuil's reply to L.98, can be read from two different viewpoints: we can imagine how impressed the conventional Mme de Volanges (with the skeleton in her cupboard) will be by arguments which are faultlessly moralistic; at the same time the

55

knowledge that they are motivated merely by Merteuil's desire to avoid forfeiting her revenge on Gercourt leaves us ironically detached. It is a fitting irony that Mme de Volanges, who is something of a hypocrite herself, should appear impressed by such hypocritical arguments (e.g. F297-8). [18]

Even that upright man of the cloth Père Anselme, unconsciously encourages Valmont to go for a quick seduction of Mme de Tourvel. In L.123, Anselme writes:

> Cependant, Monsieur le Vicomte, permettez-moi de vous inviter à ne pas différer [sc. the meeting with the Présidente] sans de fortes raisons, afin de pouvoir vous livrer plus tôt et plus entièrement aux dispositions louables que vous me témoignez. (F352-3)

'Dispositions louables' is rather rich, given what we have gathered (F335) and what we will discover of Valmont's real intentions. It is with justifiable irony that the Vicomte remarks to Merteuil (L.125, F359): 'Vous verrez [...] avec quel zèle le saint personnage s'est employé pour nous réunir'. Anselme [19] therefore demonstrates the same blindness as Danceny, who in L.93 emotionally blackmails Cécile into cooperating with Valmont, thus bringing about his own cuckolding, and making himself the butt of Valmont's ironic remark in L.96:

> J'étais bien aise, je l'avoue, d'avoir ainsi changé de rôle, et que le jeune homme fît pour moi ce qu'il comptait que je ferais pour lui. (F269)

As regards dramatic irony, Danceny is something of a special case. L.113 is a clear statement by Mme de Merteuil of her determination that Danceny is to be her new lover (F331), for, she says:

> il n'a que les grâces de la jeunesse, et non la frivolité. Sa grande réserve dans le cercle est très propre à éloigner tous les soupçons, et on ne l'en trouve que plus aimable, quand il se livre, dans le tête-a-tête. Ce n'est pas que j'en aie déjà

eu avec lui pour mon compte, je ne suis encore que sa confidente; mais *sous ce voile de l'amitié*, je crois *lui voir un goût très vif pour moi*, et je sens que *j'en prends beaucoup pour lui*. Ce serait bien dommage que tant d'esprit et de délicatesse allassent se sacrificier et s'abrutir auprès de *cette petite imbécile de Volanges* ! (*ibid.,* my italics)

We know that Merteuil is sexually attracted to Danceny (or determined to be so, if that offends Valmont), and contemptuous of Cécile. It is the privileged possession of this knowledge which enables us to treat the naively blind declarations of Danceny to Cécile in L.116 with amused contempt. In L.116, Danceny says of the Marquise:

> Mon Dieu! que cette femme est aimable! et quel charme flatteur elle sait donner à l'amitié! Il semble que ce doux sentiment s'embellisse et se fortifie chez elle de *tout ce qu'elle refuse à l'amour* [so she has no designs on him, Danceny thinks!—see the end of L.121, F349]. Si vous saviez *comme elle vous aime* , comme elle se plaît à m'entendre lui parler de vous! [...] C'est là sans doute *ce qui m'attache autant à elle* . (F339, my italics)

Thus a startling dramatic irony paves the way for a neat piece of self-deception.

One move in Valmont's end-play with Mme de Merteuil is L.155 from the Vicomte to Danceny. We read this with the same pleasure as we read L.104, seeing the plausible surface argument, persuasive enough but giving no hint of the hidden motivation beneath. Not realising that he is merely a pawn in a tactical battle, Danceny, in L.157, decides to desert Mme de Merteuil and meet the "innocent" Cécile instead—"innocent", that is, only in so far as Valmont's high-class pimping technique (L.155, F435) makes her appear so. The reader knows that Cécile has been thoroughly whored by Valmont. In these circumstances, L.157, Danceny's reply to Valmont, is a masterpiece of irony. He will go back to Cécile, he says, but:

> ménageons sa délicatesse, et cachons-lui mes torts; non

57

> pour la surprendre [an elegant hypocrisy, indeed], mais
> pour ne pas l'affliger. (F439) [20]

This concern not to offend Cécile's supposed sensibilities strikes us as ironic to the point of being positively ludicrous. Of course Danceny has to be totally in the dark thus far, so that when the scales are made to fall from his eyes later (L.162), the shock will cause him to challenge Valmont to a duel. But Danceny is here actually asking the man who has made Cécile unfaithful to him and concealed that fact from him, to conceal from the girl Danceny's own infidelities to Cécile with Mme de Merteuil, as if the "blameless" Cécile might otherwise be shocked to the very marrow. The irony could not be more piquant. And ironically Danceny expects pardon from the Marquise for deserting her and providing Valmont with his revenge:

> Je connais mon amie [Merteuil]; elle est honnête autant
> qu'indulgente [!]; elle fera plus que me pardonner, elle
> m'approuvera [!!]. (F439)

To cap it all, Danceny ends his letter with these stunningly precious good wishes:

> Mme de Tourvel reste donc inexorable ? [the Chevalier is a
> little out of date]. On la dit aussi bien malade. Mon Dieu,
> que je vous plains! Puisse-t-elle reprendre à la fois de la
> santé et de l'indulgence, et faire à jamais votre bonheur!
> (F440)

We see that he is totally blind to the true state of affairs, and the dramatic ironies now come thick and fast; from this point in the book onward Laclos's intention evidently is to ensure that every one of his characters becomes their target.

*****

Let us now attempt a summary, while bearing in mind that the boundaries of the categories of irony in question are not sharply defined, and there is always some overlapping from one to the next.

Simple irony is the natural mode of Valmont and Merteuil: like a character in Heinrich Böll's *Billiards at Half-past Nine* , the Marquise and her partner 'keep [their] superiority feelings fresh in a refrigerator of irony.'[21] It enables them to assert their alternative values and prop up their self-esteem, it confers a witty, spurious nobility on their schemes, it dramatises the gap between illusion and reality in the minds of their victims. Dramatic irony is most frequently the irony which overtakes those whom they trick, all those, in other words, who are not privy to this strained manneristic elegance of confidence and planning. Irony of plot is the irony of events that deceive the deceivers, that hounds the manipulators no less than their victims, and strips their gilded plans bare of pretension. That no major characters should escape the barbs of irony, and particularly not those who thought that they had forever at their disposal a weapon whose verbal shafts they had themselves sharpened and perfected, is proof enough—if proof be needed—that Laclos's moral is the deeply pessimistic moral of the true satirist who at every turn sees the folly of human ambition, vulnerable blindness and inconsistency, and never misses his aim.

Structure

C'est un métier que de faire un livre comme de faire une pendule:
il faut plus que de l'esprit pour être auteur.

(La Bruyère)

In form, *Les Liaisons dangereuses* is a letter novel, with all the
opportunities for exploiting the multiple viewpoint, with its extremes of
blindness and clarity, dramatic irony, ironic juxtapositions and
contrasts, which Laclos so cleverly engineers. The action of the novel
is precipitated to a large extent by the manipulations of the two main
characters, the effectiveness of whose schemes the reader is well placed
to assess in the letters of their unseeing victims: thus, for example,
Valmont's designs on the Présidente (L.23, F81; L.70, F185; L.90;
L.96, F267-8; L.99 etc.) form one coherent line of development. While
the fiction is that Valmont and Merteuil are in control of events with the
"editor" only commenting occasionally from the sidelines, the general
design, proportions and management of the plot, and the aesthetically
satisfying symmetrical patterns which all the characters' love affairs
create, betray the hand of a controlling master: Laclos.

A: Plot

The exposition in the opening chapters of *Les Liaisons* is a concise
deployment of all the information the reader needs to understand the
relationships between the dramatis personae and to find his interest in
their situation and his curiosity about possible future developments
truly aroused. (In fact, the imparting of information necessary for our
apprehension of events is always done in varied and naturalistic ways.)

The dénouement, with its theatrical compression, [1] is equally effective. Valmont's and the Présidente's deaths, Merteuil's loss of her lawsuit, her disfigurement by smallpox, her social ostracism and flight to Holland, Cécile and Danceny's withdrawal from the world to pay for their sins—events pile up on one another in quick succession and with the unrelenting inevitability of the resolution of a classical French tragedy. The central plot itself could be described as "variations on the theme of revenge", as we argued in the introductory chapter to this study. [2] Like a seventeenth-century tragedy, *Les Liaisons* possesses unity of action, it is clear, while from one viewpoint the plot can be seen as a series of parallel moves and manipulations aimed at striking a balance between the respective powers of the chief rivals, which develops into a direct confrontation in which that balance is finally overthrown.

Within the framework of the plot, nothing is irrelevant. Even the anecdotes (Valmont's 'réchauffé' with the Vicomtesse de M***, the story of Prévan's triple affair, and of his encounter with Mme de Merteuil), which may at first sight seem like digressions from the main lines of the plot, [3] are related to it and to the topic of rivalry (for example the subtlety of L.85 is intended to surpass that of L.71), and serve to give the impression of time passing during which, unconsciously, in the background so to speak, the Présidente's love for Valmont blossoms and grows and Danceny's sense of frustration in his affair with Cécile increases.[4] Moreover, if the sleeping arrangements in L.71[5] and the inevitable outcome ingeniously foreshadow Valmont's later role as the intruder between Gercourt and Danceny, who successfully beds Cécile, Prévan's 'triple affaire' reminds us of Valmont's three-way relationship with Cécile, Tourvel and Merteuil (v. L.133). A certain similarity between F241-2 and F201-202 makes it evident that if the Présidente is the weak victim, the Marquise will be the strong-willed predator, while with trembling hands (L.85, F241)

Merteuil can mimic the effect of true passion which, in Tourvel, is uncontrollable (L.23, F79). Valmont's answer to the "feminine wiles" of L.85 is the "powerfully masculine" seduction of Cécile (F269), and the highly theatrical performance described in L.125 is his attempt to disprove L.81 (F219-20) and to better Merteuil's stage-managed seduction of Prévan. To Valmont's warning to the Marquise about Prévan and his plan (F184) corresponds L.113, a month later, where she gives Valmont notice of rumours surrounding his entanglement with Mme de Tourvel (F325-6). His ploy of giving credibility to his request for an interview with Tourvel by making it through a priest (L.123) is anticipated by Merteuil's using a bishop as a third party to her opening conversations with Prévan—'un témoin respectable qui pût, au besoin, déposer de ma conduite et de mes discours' (F239). The Prévan episode could be viewed as a speeded-up advance parody, not only of the seducing of Tourvel but also of its aftermath—Merteuil takes to her bed afterwards as a result of "being ill-used" by this man, and thus prefigures Tourvel's illness after her desertion.

The rivalry theme is pursued with such skill that Laclos's filigree work in fine detail comes as a constant revelation. For instance, it is interesting to compare references to the bell-rope in L.85 and L.96 (F247 and F270), and to the 'escalier dérobé' in L.85 (F244) and the 'petit escalier' in L.156 (F438), the latter Letter 156 being drafted by Valmont who is clearly not averse to taking a leaf out of the Marquise's book. Compare, too, the "scientific" vocabulary and presentation of the two rivals in L.81 (F224, F225) and L.133 (F383-4) (and see also F271). All this is textual evidence that the Vicomte is attempting to prove himself the equal of Mme de Merteuil. It can be argued that Merteuil, for her part, makes Danceny her "pupil" (L.151), not only because Valmont prefers Tourvel to her ('temps de disette'—L.115, F336—and 'la saison morte'—L.133, F383—though unreliable explanations, make the reader aware of how the affairs run parallel), but also because Valmont has taken over the "education" of Cécile (L.96 ff.), even if in accordance with the Marquise's plans. It is notable that in L.106 *Valmont* becomes the 'Ecolier', F307, and, as far as Cécile's "treatment" is concerned, Merteuil changes the metaphor from an educational to a medical one, before finally returning to 'notre commune Pupille.' [6] References to 'élèves' 'écoliers' and 'écolières' are a consistent part of the vocabulary of rivalry.

The plot is arranged with care; letters conveying characters' plans and decisions are carefully positioned, and major events are foreshadowed in small but significant ways. Gercourt's letter putting off his marriage with Cécile comes early, because the marriage has to be delayed two months to suit the time scheme of the dénouement (see L.170, F463). A trip to the country by Merteuil is seen as a possibility already in L.87; the Marquise leaves Paris early, ostensibly to get rid of Belleroche by boring him with excessive devotion (L.113, F330), but in fact so as not to be in Paris when Valmont returns. [7] This enables Laclos to introduce the theme of Merteuil's lawsuit early (F330-1, echoing the earlier 'grand procès' which drove a wedge between the Présidente and her husband in L.4). Thus the loss of the court case later does not appear as an unlikely contrivance, which is part of some makeshift, bogus morality imposed upon the ending. Conversely, when the Marquise leaves for the country in L.113 there is no mention of an epidemic of smallpox in the neighbourhood: this means that her disfigurement comes all the more effectively like a bolt from the blue, [8] and there can be no question of her persuading Danceny, supposing this were possible after the revelations of the correspondence Valmont gives him (L.163), to accompany her into exile as some saving consolation. Valmont's scheme with Père Anselme as his catspaw comes as a bombshell (L.125, F359), but in retrospect we realise that Valmont is only exploiting uninventively (compare F307 and F335) an idea suggested by L.51 and by L.107, F312, not to mention the reference to the bishop in L.85. Moreover, since Valmont causes Tourvel to love him by flattering her with the illusion that she can convert him from his libertine ways, his use of her confessor to gain access to her house in order to seduce her is simply an extension of this ploy. Just as the duel in which Valmont is killed, in effect for insulting Merteuil (v. L.158), is faintly prefigured by the mention of the possibility that Belleroche might be provoked to challenge Prévan for his supposed insult to Merteuil's honour (L.85, F248), so also the eventual retreat to a convent of the Présidente and of Cécile is foreshadowed by the outcome for one of the women participants in Prévan's notorious affair (L.79, F215), and by the threat Mme de Volanges makes when she discovers Danceny's love letters to Cécile (L.63, F168). The reconciliation of Prévan with his three rivals (L.79, F213-214) is a foretaste of what happens between Danceny and Valmont after *their* duel.

B: Patterning

On a very general level, the minor characters appear as lesser versions of the major ones in *Les Liaisons* . The Marquise and the Vicomte being the great libertines and manipulators of the novel, others with some of the same pretensions will be no more than pale imitations of them. Danceny, for example, abandoning Cécile to pursue Merteuil, seems to be a kind of Valmont *manqué* .[9] In L.155, by ironically playing upon the idea of the unscrupulous young libertine that the Chevalier has become, Valmont can manoeuvre Danceny into casting off a demeaning self-image, definitively choosing the one who is his true love, thus abandoning Merteuil in the desired insulting way. Valmont asks:

> ...le Danceny d'aujourd'hui, arraché par les femmes,
> courant les aventurers, et devenu, suivant l'usage, un peu

> scélérat, préférera-t-il une jeune fille timide, qui n'a pour
> elle que sa beauté, son innocence et son amour, aux
> agréments d'une femme parfaitement *usagée* ?

Then he adds:

> Pour moi, mon cher ami, il me semble que, même dans
> vos nouveaux principes, que j'avoue bien être aussi un peu
> les miens [cp. F51, F357], les circonstances me
> décideraient pour la jeune Amante. D'abord, c'en est une /
> de plus, et puis la nouveauté, et encore la crainte de perdre
> le fruit de vos soins en négligeant de le cueillir...(F435-6)

Just as Valmont tricked Danceny into unknowingly helping him to
seduce Cécile (L.96), now he manoeuvres Danceny into making love to
Cécile in order to prove he is not a libertine (L.157, F439), but
Merteuil has the edge in manipulation, for Valmont's seduction of
Cécile was all part of her plan (L.63). It is her revelation of L.96 to
Danceny which precipitates the duel (L.162). The egregious Danceny,
this 'homme à bonnes fortunes' in the words of the Vicomte (F434), is
no more than a pawn in the final battle of the rivals, who is merely
given the illusion that he is a free agent pursuing the woman he
chooses.[10]

Similarly, Mme de Volanges is perhaps a sort of Merteuil *manquée* .
Early in the book she is simultaneously something of a hypocrite and a
would-be manipulator (compare Merteuil in L.104). The Marquise's
disclosures about her past (L.106, F309) help to explain Mme de
Volanges's moralistic intervention in Tourvel's private life in Letters 9
and 32, but while Merteuil can twist Mme de Volanges round her little
finger with her combination of careful flattery and conservative
morality in L.104, the latter, despite some perceptive but second-hand
comment in L.32, cannot make Mme de Tourvel do as she advises. The
Marquise can change her tack when it suits her purpose (v. L.105,
F304-5, and cp. the end of L.38, F113), but Mme de Volanges does
not possess the flexibility which makes for an effective manipulator;

having warned the Présidente against Valmont from the very beginning she cannot change course in L.154, and therefore can do nothing to effect a life-saving reconciliation between the two lovers, though Valmont, in one version, gave her the perfect moral alibi (see Appendix, F493). Mme de Volanges ends the book aware that her advice to the Présidente was of no avail, and as uncertain of what to do with her daughter in L.170 (F463) as she was in L.98. Merteuil is nothing if not sure of herself (too sure of herself, ultimately).[11]

Even the servants as lesser versions of their masters reflect and thereby highlight traits and roles of the foreground characters. Azolan is a resourceful schemer who makes love to order—see L.101, F290: 'vous serez dans le cas de bien d'autres, qui valent mieux que vous'—in much the same way as Valmont, who cannot help appearing to be merely following instructions when he "debauches" Cécile (L.106, F308), and Azolan, for fear of being overheard, has already taken Julie to his own room to seduce her (L.44), just as the Vicomte will Cécile (L.110). Victoire is a schemer for Mme de Merteuil and her satellite (v., for example, L.63, F169), because she is in a position to be blackmailed by the Marquise (v. L.81, F229), just as Merteuil herself is at the mercy of a Valmont in possession of L.81. Père Anselme has the same strengths and weaknesses as Mme de Tourvel: the same attachment to religion, the same lack of insight into Valmont's true motives in asking for a final meeting, the same naive trust in his "conversion". The Présidente's servant Julie has two lovers, exactly like Cécile (v. F127 and F290; cp. F317).

*****

Much more striking are the parallels between Cécile and the Présidente in their love affairs.[12] Just as Cécile ignores the advice of Sophie Carnay and becomes entangled in an exchange of letters with

Danceny (L.18 and L.19; L.29 and L.30), so the Présidente becomes involved with Valmont, and, willy-nilly, maintains a correspondence with him despite Mme de Volanges's warnings. Cécile fails to realise that her tears (L.14) are a sign of her growing love for Danceny; the Présidente is equally blind to the evidence of her increasing emotional interest in Valmont, as is clear from the unconscious admission of her jealousy of Merteuil (L.11, F58). The Vicomte's disingenuous 'Hélas! je cherchais à combattre un penchant que je sentais devenir plus fort que moi' (L.36, F109) echoes Cécile's 'mais il [Danceny] dit que c'était plus fort que lui' (L.27, F89). No less than Letters 11 to 14, the close proximity of Letters 26 and 27, and 49 and 50, draws the reader's attention to the comparable position of the two women. On two occasions Cécile attempts to break off with Danceny (L.19 and L.49). Cécile, in L.27 (F89), explains to Mme de Merteuil that she wrote to Danceny 'en partie, pour lui dire de ne plus écrire'; in the very letter previous, Mme de Tourvel has told Valmont to commit the expression of his feelings to the 'silence qu'il me semble avoir droit d'attendre, et même d'exiger de vous' (L.26, F88). In two consecutive letters (49 and 50) both women impose silence upon their suitors; the Présidente talks of her 'devoir' (F141), Cécile of her 'bonne résolution' (F139). Scruples of conscience lead them both to show severity towards their respective lovers at the same point in the book.

The parallel between the two affairs is made more obvious because Valmont and Danceny use the same gambits, while their partners exhibit the same tendency at times—when Cécile rises above her usual naivety, that is—to have recourse to the tortuous, over-sophisticated arguments of lovers. Compare accusations of pitilessness L.24, F83 and L.28, F91, and note the same insistence by the men on a vital distinction between love and friendship (L.28, F91, L.29 and L.30, F93 and F94; L.67, F180, and L.68, F181); Danceny's comments on the 'vil séducteur [qui] peut plier ses projets aux circonstances' (L.64,

F173) anticipate Valmont's double-bluff in the third paragraph of L.68, F181, while both men refuse to hand back letters (L.35 and L.64) and there is the same talk of 'preuves' (L.20 and L.53); Cécile and Tourvel tie themselves in knots in a not dissimilar way—cp. the ends of L.16 and of L.102 (F65-6, and F294). All lovers, of course, talk the same language and experience similar problems and feelings, but Laclos underlines not the universality of passion but the special character of the parallel affairs which dominate his plot when, in L.57, he has Valmont draw a provocative analogy between the slowness of a naive first lover and the slowness of a libertine in love: 'entre la conduite de Danceny avec la petite Volanges, et la mienne avec la prude Mme de Tourvel, il n'y a que la différence du plus au moins' (F157). Mme de Merteuil's unsuccessful plan (L.51), in which the supposed obligation on a penitent and reformed Cécile to meet Danceny and return his love letters is intended as an opportunity for Danceny to seduce the girl, is mirrored in Valmont's later unerring ploy to gain an interview with Mme de Tourvel on the pretext of returning *her* letters, but in fact in order to seduce her (L.120). Both episodes involve a conversation with a father-confessor and an intended seduction.

Both Cécile and the Présidente are compared to Mary Magdalene: when Mme de Tourvel nearly succumbs to her passion for Valmont in L.99 we are reminded how like the type of repentant sinner she is (see F283), and the whole emotional scene irresistibly recalls the earlier one, as described by Merteuil, in which Cécile had played the chief role (see L.63, F169). The emotional storm leaves visible after-effects in the Présidente's case (see F284), and her haggard look after nearly giving in is more than a little reminiscent of Cécile's 'mine de lendemain' after the girl has actually capitulated to Valmont (L.96, F272).[13] While Mme de Volanges misinterprets Cécile's changed appearance as being the result of her daughter's pining for Danceny (L.98, F276), back in her own home, to which she has fled to save herself from Valmont, the Présidente misconstrues Valmont's apparent ill-health as the consequence of his missing her, when in fact the Vicomte, in an Ovidian fashion, is simply playing upon his exhaustion from nights in bed with Cécile (L.110—L.114).[14] Both Cécile and the Présidente change their confidantes as a result of a moral failing. Faced with the fact of her love, Mme de Tourvel cannot continue to correspond with Mme de Volanges who has warned her of that very danger, and chooses the unexacting Mme de Rosemonde to confide in (L.102); Cécile cannot keep up the schoolgirl chatter with the innocent, cloistered Sophie Carnay after the first night with Valmont, and so falls into the trap of telling her shameful secrets to the positively corrupting Mme de Merteuil (L.97). Both Cécile de Volanges and Tourvel are seduced and become the victims of the Vicomte's manipulation through his exploiting the trust they place in men—Cécile in Danceny (see L.93, and L.96, F269); the Présidente in Père Anselme—and both men unwittingly encourage Valmont's plans (see L.93 and L.123, F352-3). Both women end their lives in a convent (L.147 and L.170). On one level this sustained parallel no doubt suggests that virtue cannot, any more than all-too-easily-corruptible innocence, resist the wiles of a *roué;* [15] yet it is pursued in such detail and with such care that the first impression we receive is of an author's sheer delight in self-sufficing patterning, balance, and fine workmanship.

Thus the parallel couples become a trio, with Danceny eliminated and the Vicomte, with economical symmetry, running two affairs in tandem (an outcome perhaps already hinted at through the parallel in Valmont's delivery of love letters: compare L.25 and L.76). But the network of analogies does not stop there. The Merteuil-Danceny amour runs parallel to, and is a by-product of, the Valmont-Cécile liaison. For Danceny, a sexual relationship with the Marquise is, without him realising it, compensation for his failure to take Cécile to bed, in the same way that Valmont's night games with the young Volanges make amends for his inability to bed the Présidente: v. L.110, F320 [16] —luckily Cécile and Danceny are both able to dissociate love and pleasure, the demands of the heart and those of the body.[17] If Valmont is to replace Merteuil as Cécile's sexual tutor, then the Marquise will perform a similar service for Danceny. Mme de Merteuil, who makes the first advances—though Danceny is too blind to see this—is provocatively prepared to accept the Chevalier as her lover if Valmont is delayed with the Présidente or a replacement, and her correspondence with Danceny echoes that of Tourvel with Valmont. [18] At least three characters make do with what amount to substitute lovers, however they choose to paint them.

By L.125, Valmont has brought his pursuit of the Présidente to a successful conclusion; in accordance with her promise made in L.20, his reward from Merteuil now falls due. The Marquise and the Vicomte are now each involved in a triangular relationship with, respectively, Valmont and Danceny, and Merteuil and Tourvel. Whether or not the usual sexual rivalry and jealousy typical of the "eternal triangle" are operative, and the precise motivation behind the byzantine manoeuvres of the protagonists in those letters which follow L.125, are matters for clarification in the next chapter; what is obvious is that this is an inherently unstable state of "affairs" which demands simplification. To maintain a just equilibrium, one partner in each triangle has to be removed: in fact the scene is set for Valmont and Merteuil to eliminate each other.

After Valmont has seduced Tourvel and claimed his reward from Merteuil, some of the gambits employed when the Marquise argues against the renewal of a permanent lovers' relationship between herself and the Vicomte—as if enticing Valmont to prove her wrong—bear a close resemblance to attitudes struck in Mme de Tourvel's earlier letters to Valmont. For instance, at the end of her L.131 to Valmont, looking back with alluring nostalgia on the past, the Marquise says (F380):

> Dans le temps où nous nous aimions, car je crois que c'était de l'amour, j'étais heureuse; et vous, Vicomte ?... Mais pourquoi s'occuper encore d'un bonheur qui ne peut revenir? Non, quoi que vous en disiez, c'est un retour impossible. D'abord, j'exigerais des sacrifices que sûrement vous ne pourriez ou ne voudriez pas me faire [i.e. Valmont's giving up the Présidente; his permanent fidelity to the Marquise] [...] et puis, comment vous fixer ?

These comments may perhaps remind us of the end of L.50 from Mme de Tourvel to Valmont, a letter which rejects the idea that love can guarantee happiness and insists on the inevitability of his inconstancy and attraction to other women. It is in L.50 that the Présidente declares:

> je me connais bien peu de moyens de plaire: je les aurais tous, que je ne les croirais pas suffisants pour vous fixer. (F141)

Continuing on the same tack, in L.134 the Marquise tells Valmont: 'Croyez-moi, ne soyons qu'amis, et restons-en là' (F387), as if recalling the earlier dispute over the distinction between love and friendship and aping Mme de Tourvel's own words to Valmont in L.67:

> Pour me livrer à ce sentiment si doux, si bien fait pour mon cœur [l'amitié], je n'attends que votre aveu; et la parole, que j'exige de vous, que cette amitié suffira à votre bonheur. (F180)

If the Vicomte indulges in the same false language of compliment to the Marquise as much earlier to Mme de Tourvel (cp. 'régner seule sur mon âme', F147, and 'la véritable souveraine de mon cœur', F375) then the Marquise will employ the same language of refusal as Tourvel: but more successfully. The effect on Valmont of these ironic echoes of phrases and arguments from the past subtly underlines the fact that the Marquise's power to control and manipulate him is superior to that of the Présidente.

Of course the renewal of the old affair of Valmont and Merteuil must remain impossible if Valmont continues to be emotionally attached to the Présidente and if the Marquise has perversely chosen Danceny as a replacement for Belleroche. Theoretically 'une infidélité réciproque' would be necessary if Merteuil and Valmont were to renew their alliance, or rather, fulfil the contract of L.20—the sacrifice of Belleroche and Danceny on the one side would equal and counter-balance the sacrifice of Cécile and the Présidente on the other—but if Valmont remains besotted with Mme de Tourvel then his pledges and compliments to Merteuil (at the end of L.129 and of L.133) must sound as hollow as some of his justifications. He tells Merteuil, for example, that he renewed relations with the Présidente, broken off by the latter after the escapade with Emilie, because 'j'ai voulu vous réserver l'honneur de ce sacrifice'(L.138, F397), and even the supposedly clinching proof of his dedication to Merteuil (L.142) is nullified in his very next letter to her by his reluctance to consider the affair with Tourvel to be over. If the Marquise, therefore, regards his preference for the Présidente as humiliating (L.145, F412)—just as Mme de Tourvel complained when he deserted her for Emilie: 'Tout ce qu'on peut réunir d'infortunes, d'humiliations, je les éprouve, et c'est de lui qu'elles me viennent' (L.135, F389)—Valmont likewise will regard Merteuil's preference for Danceny as equally mortifying (L.151, F427), and the former partners become locked in a pattern of mutual revenge which leads to mutual destruction.

In the projected renewal of the Valmont-Merteuil affair, as in the Valmont-Présidente affair, there is therefore the same idea of humiliation and sacrifice. Valmont's sacrifice of Mme de Tourvel, which the Marquise had after all herself suggested (L.134, F387-8), ought, in natural justice, to be compensated for by Merteuil's sacrifice of Danceny. In L.151 Valmont urges Merteuil:

> Surtout, plus de Danceny. [...]
> J'espère même que ce sacrifice ne vous en paraîtra pas un.
> Mais quand il vous coûterait quelque chose, il me semble
> que je vous ai donné un assez bel exemple! qu'une femme
> sensible et belle [Mme de Tourvel], qui n'existait que pour
> moi, qui dans ce moment même meurt peut-être d'amour et
> de regret, peut bien valoir un jeune écolier. (F427)

In L.131, Merteuil had already insinuated to Valmont—of course with
no intention of keeping her word—that she was ready to sacrifice
Danceny after first winning him:

> vous voyez bien que ce ne serait pas là [Belleroche] un
> sacrifice à vous faire! Une infidélité réciproque rendra le
> charme bien plus puissant. (F380)

Without true sacrifices on both sides a mutual accommodation
between the old lovers is impossible, and if not 'love'—then *war* !
(L.153), but if Valmont has failed to repay the Présidente's sacrifice of
her honour by unswerving fidelity, then how can he legitimately
complain if Merteuil seemingly wishes to remain faithful to Danceny
and is unwilling to sacrifice him for Valmont, particularly if the latter's
sacrifice of Tourvel seems only provisional ? (To imply the necessity
for the sacrifice of a rival and then to complain in the name of rejected
women when it is made is no doubt a woman's privilege). To talk of
'la grandeur des sacrifices' that 'un cœur neuf et sensible' would be
obliged to make for love, as the Présidente had done (L.50, F140, and
cp. the end of L.78), referring to the breaking of her marital vow of
fidelity, is no exaggeration: 'c'est pour lui [Valmont] que je me suis
perdue' (L.128, F372)—and it is all for nothing if Valmont is prepared
to sacrifice Tourvel to his vanity (L.142; L.145).

There is the same talk of "power" and "charm", too. The power
which Valmont pretends Mme de Tourvel exercises over him (see L.58
and the end paragraph of L.83, particularly the phrase 'Ah! Madame,
de grâce, n'abusez pas de votre empire!', F234) he acknowledges to be

a real enough threat in *Merteuil* 's case, when he discovers the latter has tricked him (see the end of L.145 and the beginning of L.146): 'Reconnaissez là votre empire; mais croyez-moi, contente de l'avoir éprouvé, n'en abusez pas plus longtemps' (L.151, F427, and cp. F388). To this the Marquise responds with a counter-claim: 'Vous désirez moins mes bontés, que vous ne voulez abuser de votre empire' (L.152, F429). L.83, F232-3, twice mentions the "charm" that Valmont tells the Présidente she lends to the virtues which she displays, and in the letter where he describes his seduction of her, much is made of the 'charme inconnu' he experienced (L.125 F357)—an attraction which Mme de Merteuil is determined to find so objectionable (L.127, F370 and see L.129). If Valmont discovers charm in another woman, it is fitting that Merteuil will be unable to detect that quality in the Vicomte, who, in his high-handed approach, so singularly fails to resemble the charming Valmont of old (L.152, F430).

*****

The discovery of these patterns has led some critics to describe the action of the book as a ballet or dance. There is, as it were, a background quadrille between the two couples Merteuil-Valmont and Cécile-Danceny, with the Marquise linking with Danceny after Valmont has joined up with Cécile; while in the foreground is a pas de deux performed by the Vicomte and the Présidente in which the two partners are seen together first of all in the château of Mme de Rosemonde, Valmont goes away, then the two come together again when he returns; next the Présidente runs away back to her home, then finally the two are seen together in Paris, where Valmont seduces her.[19] Loosely developing some of Seylaz's ideas about the book's dance-like structure, Philip Thody states:

the action in *Les Liaisons dangereuses* is almost like a ballet, in which Mme de Merteuil is always trying to replace La Présidente as Valmont's leading partner, and / succeeds for a time, before ending the dance by suddenly refusing to keep to the same rhythm, in interposing herself between Cécile and Danceny. In this formal dance, La Présidente and Cécile both have something of the same rôle, both seduced by Valmont while trying to remain faithful to someone else, both sharing him without knowing it *before finally losing him to Mme de Merteuil* , and even taking the same number of "steps" in the sense that they both write twenty-four letters. [20]

But when exactly does Cécile lose Valmont to *Mme de Merteuil* : L.134 ? L.140 ? L.158 ? It is not certain that Valmont redirects Danceny away from Merteuil and back to Cécile, L.155, primarily so that he can himself return to Merteuil.[21] No doubt the idea of the book as a dance of characters would be entirely appropriate if motivation could be discarded as irrelevant to a purely ritual process where patterns are created for the sake of creating patterns. To talk of *Les Liaisons* as dance captures something of the strong ludic element which is undoubtedly there, but perhaps gives a false impression of a world of superficial gallantry where partners are exchanged with a casual abandon, a world where calculating pride, emotional imbroglio and their destructive consequences cannot impinge. Ultimately the elegant intertwining patterns which make up the rich texture of the work are more than merely decorative: for the characters concerned they form a *fatal* symmetry. The patterns made are not aesthetically self-sufficient and simply for display; they are moves in a deadly game ("design" in a double sense), and Merteuil's choice of, and unwavering adherence to, Danceny as her final partner is a deliberate part of the end-play, yet a move whose ultimate consequences leave her with fewer choices and less control than she anticipated. When Valmont realises that his sacrifice of Tourvel is fruitless, Merteuil's dedication to her new partner is revealed as more than a playful challenge, and the

Vicomte will do all he can to separate her from her young suitor and thus remove her advantage. The Marquise, who has invested all her pride and self-respect in her continual possession of Danceny and refusal of Valmont, will be forced to overplay her hand. In this game of poker or chess the stakes could not be higher: reputation, *amour-propre,* a certain conception of personal honour and glory, however remote from the idealism of its Cornelian origins—all these things are in play, and for characters who have rejected all other values but these, the game, in the final analysis, is a matter of life and death.

Chess, perhaps, provides a more appropriate analogy than dance to describe the final exchanges of the novel. [22] Lacking a long-term strategy, and as bad a defensive player as he is full of illusions about his ability to capture and recapture whichever queen he chooses, [23] Valmont loses his touch and is outmanoeuvred. But Merteuil's triumph in L.145 is premature; there is an outcome unknown in chess—a double checkmate. Merteuil may be rash but right to surmise that the outraged sense of betrayed trust of her pawn Danceny (should we promote him to the position of knight ?) will turn him into an inspired duellist, but she is both rash and wrong not to have chosen any other method of revenge but a duel for Valmont's final insult (L.158).

In order to understand the end-play of the book, however, we shall have to look more closely at the Valmont-Merteuil relationship and at the mutual assumptions on which it is based.

Valmont and Merteuil

Les Liaisons dangereuses ... cette sombre planche
d'anatomie morale.

(Paul Bourget)

Is it possible to devise a single, consistent, continually credible line of
interpretation of the relations between Valmont and Merteuil in *Les
Liaisons dangereuses* ? Such a reading could not afford to be hedged
around with a profusion of provisos and of significant alternatives. It
should do justice to all the ambiguities of the text, without making far
too many unwarranted guesses about what Henri Duranton aptly calls
'le dessous des cartes'; [1] but also, avoid the temptation to reduce the
interplay of characters, as perhaps Duranton does, to some
psychologically shallow mechanism of rivalry which has been put on
"self-destruct".

Firstly, let us propose two summary interpretations of their
relationship, based on the opposite assumptions that the Marquise is or
is not in love with Valmont, both of which also take it that Valmont
falls in love with Mme de Tourvel. Then we will examine the
correspondence of the two rivals in more detail to test out what appears
to be the more interesting second version, analysing the sequence of
letters from L.125 onwards so as to gain a better grasp of motives and
events which lead to the dénouement and to take in the question of the
Vicomte's feelings for the Présidente.

*****

Imagine that Merteuil is all the time in love with Valmont.[2] She drafted the separation "pact" (L.4) as a means of retaining some control over him while allowing him to "wander". She is in love with the Vicomte, but she regards her love for him as a humiliating weakness. Her jealousy is aroused when he embarks on what she sees as a sentimental affair with the Présidente; [3] implying that she has no wish to play second fiddle to Tourvel and thus preserving her self-respect, she tries to attract him back as her lover by offering herself in a flippant way as a reward for his seducing and abandoning the Présidente (L.20), and she manipulates him into a liaison with Cécile more in order to try to distract him from Mme de Tourvel than so that he may serve as the instrument of her vengeance on Gercourt. Initially Valmont presents himself in danger of falling in love with Tourvel, hoping to force Merteuil into making an emotional claim on him—an admission of weakness—and renewing their affair. Ironically, he pretends to be in love with Tourvel to compel the Marquise to confess her love for him when in fact she has never stopped loving him, but falls victim to his own role-playing with the Présidente, for whom he does begin to experience hitherto unknown emotions, and pretends to be more interested in Merteuil when he is at his least credible because of this. Fortunately for her, the Marquise therefore experiences no problems in controlling her feelings for him; all along she has pointed out his love for the Présidente above all to convince herself that she, Merteuil, cannot love him (the affairs with Prévan and Danceny are no doubt the unconsciously jealous reactions of a woman who is exasperated by Valmont's prolonged amour with Tourvel just as much as they are a riposte to his anti-feminism and boasting). And because he equally regards emotional ties as degrading, an imperfection to his image, she can manoeuvre him into losing the love of his life, Tourvel, through his own stupid act (L.142), not in the hope of taking him back, but in the full knowledge (L.131) that a renewal of their affair is an impossibility.

*****

If, however, we assume Merteuil is not in love with the Vicomte, a very different view of motive and events emerges. Before the book began, Merteuil had become dissatisfied with Valmont, a man she initially waylaid to restore her self-respect after being jilted by Gercourt. Indeed, perhaps she originally attracted Valmont in order to dominate and control him because she had lost control over Gercourt. From the start her intention was to get rid of Valmont so as to allay the insult to her pride, inflicted by Gercourt's wilful and unacceptable abandonment of her, and her long-term pursuit of revenge on Gercourt perhaps means that she remains obsessed with her earlier lover. She dispatched the Vicomte in a much more subtle way than Gercourt had her. She presented the separation pact so skilfully to Valmont that she managed to break with him while allowing him to retain his self-conceit: the idea that they should separate to preach their mission of love and seduce as many lovers as possible (L.4) appealed to Valmont's vanity and sustained his self-image as a libertine, so that he was not aware of being in effect abandoned by the Marquise. But having got rid of Valmont, she takes the 'mission d'amour' seriously, since it amounts to a competition to demonstrate superiority in the skilful conduct of sexual affairs, a competition which, whether the victim be Prévan, or Danceny, or Valmont himself whom she ultimately refuses to have back as her lover, she is certain that she can win.

Valmont's greatest miscalculation is to think that Merteuil had been, and remains, in love with him. He therefore considers that he can insult her by describing the 'sentiment inconnu' evoked in him by Madame de Tourvel (Ll.57 and 125), yet the Marquise will always be prepared to accept him back as her lover. For a woman who is, as he thinks, secretly in love with him, will surely clutch at the feeble straw of his assertion of a purely "scientific" interest in the Présidente (L.133); must surely respond to the supposed proof of his love for her—his sacrifice of Tourvel (see L.142). No doubt he assumes that behind all the banter and ostentatious vanity in L.20, Merteuil made the offer which that letter contains (that he should seduce the Présidente and she would be his reward) because she was prepared to take back her old lover at any cost, even if it meant he was to be allowed to pursue another woman first. He must deludedly imagine that the Marquise hoped her offer of L.20 would be an incentive to him to speed up the process of seduction, so that she could welcome back her former lover with open arms. In reality, Merteuil conceived of the bargain of L.20 as a plan to free Valmont as soon as possible from the Présidente so that he then would have no excuse not to seduce Cécile for her: revenge on Gercourt was her priority. Merteuil's description of herself in a state of alluring undress (L.10), which seems designed to distract and entice him away from the charms of the Présidente *en déshabillé* (L.6), perhaps deceived him into thinking he detected the tactics of a jealous woman. No doubt her original plan for him to seduce Cécile was her very first attempt to sidetrack him from Tourvel: Valmont can imagine that Merteuil has guessed at his interest in the Présidente even before L.4. In L.20, the Marquise, he must think, though making a show of it, has swallowed her pride and is using another ploy to get him back. As soon as Merteuil realises that Valmont's plan to seduce Mme de Tourvel and her own plan for him to seduce Cécile are not mutually exclusive, since Valmont can, if she so arranges it (L.63, L.74, L.85), run two affairs in tandem—and she is right to have anticipated that he will fall for Cécile as a distraction from the rigours of Tourvel—she begins to look for ways of *not* abiding by the bargain of L.20, now that her purpose is achieved and Cécile is no longer the innocent virgin that Gercourt hoped for. An affair with Danceny will be the perfect excuse for her not to give Valmont his expected reward when he has seduced Mme de Tourvel (though Valmont, thinking that Merteuil is in love with him, does not take L.113 (F331) seriously).

Besides, why should the Marquise accept a 'renouvellement de bail' (L.20) with Valmont, a man she has never loved, when he couples a brutal request for his pound of flesh from her (L.125) with evidence of his love for Mme de Tourvel, only to follow it with unconvincing assertions of his love for Merteuil in L.142 ? The sacrifice of the Présidente does not prove that he holds the Marquise in greater esteem, but that vanity for the moment has triumphed over his feelings for Tourvel. Merteuil's sentimental memories of their past liaison (L.131)—often seen as evidence of her abiding love for the Vicomte—are in fact part of a series of moves (which include something akin to feigned jealousy: see L.134) [4] to force him to sacrifice Tourvel for her without there being any intention on her part to reciprocate by sacrificing Danceny. In a sense, too, Merteuil, while incapable of falling in love with Danceny (or, for that matter, anyone?),[5] at any rate has fallen in love with the idea she wishes Danceny should have of her (see the end of L.113, F332). She will not relinquish Danceny, therefore a fight to the finish with her rival is inevitable (even if the mismanagement of hostilities is not). The scene is set for the declaration of 'Hé bien! la guerre' (F432), for war is the natural culmination of their libertine competition, which Valmont had seen as a way of preserving their friendship inviolate (L.15).

Does *Les Liaisons dangereuses* chart the progress of Merteuil's finally successful efforts to dominate a secret passion for Valmont, or is it not rather the story of Merteuil's systematic fostering and exploitation of Valmont's delusion that she harbours such a passion for him ?

Relations between the pair of them have been broken off and they have remained apart ever since late July (see L.115, F334, and L.10, F53-4). Despite the exaggerated lapse of time suggested by Valmont's ironic confession 'il me semble que dans cette mission d'amour, vous avez fait plus de prosélytes que moi' (L.4, F39), the separation plan itself (*ibid.*) may be a fairly recent decision. [6] L.2 is an open invitation by Merteuil to Valmont to seduce Cécile so that she can be revenged on the former lover Gercourt who deserted her; equally it seems intended to give the impression to Valmont that in fact she has already (at last?) had a change of heart and really wants Valmont back to replace Belleroche. The use of the libertine code at the end of L.2—'bientôt je ne m'occuperai plus de vous', F37 (see V1175, n.1)—indicates to the Vicomte that Merteuil is giving him an *assignation* (at which he will supposedly receive marching orders for the campaign against Cécile). Valmont's response in L.4 is to hint at Merteuil's feelings for him in his ambivalent and possibly ironic attribution to her of the remark 'Voilà l'homme selon mon cœur' (F40), while explaining his designs on Mme de Tourvel, and his letter ends with this:

> J'ai bien besoin d'avoir cette femme pour me sauver du ridicule d'en être amoureux: car où ne mène pas un désir contrarié? [...] Que nous sommes heureux que les femmes se défendent si mal! nous ne serions auprès d'elles que de timides esclaves. J'ai dans ce moment un sentiment de reconnaissance pour les femmes faciles, qui m'amène naturellement à vos pieds. (F41)

Here, behind the sarcastic wit designed to anger Merteuil, does not Valmont really assume with chauvinistic pride that Merteuil is not the sort of woman who can make him ridiculous by thwarting his desires? He must think that she is in love with him and will accept him back as a lover at any time. Why should he think that? Either because he believes Merteuil's plan for him to go to her house for a tête-à-tête two hours before seeing Cécile (F37) is proof enough of Merteuil's wish to get him in her clutches again under the guise of giving him instructions concerning Cécile, or because Merteuil had so effectively simulated a repressed emotional, as well as shown an overt sexual, attachment to him, which must be abandoned with regret for the sake of higher libertine ends (the 'mission d'amour' mentioned in L.4, which was in reality the excuse for Merteuil to abandon Valmont before he left her).[7] Valmont's naivety in penetrating women's purposes is so apparent, e.g. in L.99, that it is hard to believe that in giving credit to the idea that Merteuil actually loves him what Valmont has detected is the truth. Seeing the war between the rivals at the end of the book following Merteuil's (engineered ?) meeting of her two suitors Danceny and Valmont in L.151, and faced with a choice between the hard-nosed realism of L.81 (with its rejection of sentimental love and its view of male-female relationships as a battle where the odds are stacked heavily in favour of men) and the seemingly romantic nostalgia of L.131, the reader is in no doubt as to what Merteuil's real feelings are. Her overall purpose in the book is not to win back the Vicomte in some way which is reconcilable with her *amour-propre* , but to revenge herself on Gercourt for his typically male, unthinking, easy desertion of her, and to win the sexual competition between herself and Valmont, manoeuvring him into a losing position by playing upon her supposed affection for him. L.4, then, is to be considered as the first sign of the Vicomte's misconception that he may with impunity be as disrespectful as he likes to the woman he mistakenly supposes to be in love with him; from this point on, Merteuil herself, who has become aware of his mistake, is ready to make all the capital she can from the impression she encouraged Valmont to form: that behind the libertine image—itself masked from the world by her social persona—can be read the true character of the woman who secretly loves him still.

Merteuil hints that she is prepared to sacrifice Belleroche (L.5, F43), the proviso that Valmont desist from his plans for the Présidente being taken as read. Her contemptuous dismissal of Tourvel's physical attractions (F42) is followed by the mention of the competitively seductive *déshabillé* (L.10). Her frantic love-making with Belleroche, with its moment of tenderness (F54) succeeded by expansive sensuality (F56), comes after Valmont has insisted on Tourvel's charms and on his emotional rejuvenation (does he think that he is insulting Merteuil by insinuating that his affair with the Marquise, no less than others more recent (?), had contributed to his 'cœur flétri', L.6, F46 ?) All this is intended to seem to the Vicomte like the reaction of a jealous woman. But Merteuil is exploiting her pretence of jealousy in order to trap Valmont into mechanically feigning jealousy of Belleroche (L.15) so that she can find a justification for making Valmont the offer of L.20, which aims to free him for the work of revenge. No doubt Merteuil's allegations (L.10) that he is in love with Tourvel appear to him to be charged with the barely suppressed indignation of a spurned woman, who, as he sees it, will even be prepared to incite him to seduce the Présidente quickly so that he will avoid a long-term emotional entanglement. However, in the same way that Valmont's criticisms of Merteuil's indulgent treatment of Belleroche (L.15, F63: 'Que ferait de plus son esclave ?') simply re-echo the image of the harem already suggested by the Marquise (L.10, F56), these charges develop ideas that Valmont had already provided her with (see L.4, F41: 'J'ai bien besoin d'avoir cette femme, pour me sauver du ridicule d'en être amoureux'), but as part of a strategy to remove the Vicomte from the Présidente's spell and redirect him towards Cécile as soon as pleasure has taken the blindfold from love's eyes (L.6, F44).

The description in L.10 of the night in the *petite maison* produces the desired result: Valmont is supposedly overcome with envy at Belleroche's good fortune—'savez-vous que vous m'avez rendu jaloux de lui ?' (L.15, F62). It hardly matters that his resentment at the special favours granted to the *régnant Chevalier* does not appear genuine [8] (for, after all, a *cœur flétri* can have little interest in this spectacular sexual display)—the mere simulation of jealousy is enough to give Merteuil the lever she wants, and she can challenge Valmont to prove her wrong in her intuition about 'le petit chagrin que cela [her treatment of Belleroche] vous cause' (L.20) by quickly dispatching Tourvel.

In L.15, Valmont accuses the Marquise of being Belleroche's slave because she had accused him in effect of being enslaved by Tourvel: he suspects her of only pretending to be especially devoted to Belleroche because she is jealous of his predilection for the Présidente. The second paragraph of this letter may be a private parody of what Valmont fancies to be the train of thought running through Merteuil's head: this becomes clearer when we reverse the terms and imagine that it is Merteuil who is speaking:

> Mais que vous vous donniez entièrement à *une d'elles* ! qu'il existe *une autre femme* [i.e. Tourvel] aussi heureuse que moi! je ne le souffrirai pas; n'espérez pas que je le souffre. Ou reprenez-moi, ou au moins prenez-en *une autre* [i.e. Cécile]; et ne trahissez pas, par un caprice exclusif, l'amitié inviolable que nous nous sommes jurée. (F63)

Valmont may think he is being privately ironic in striking an attitude the mirror-image of what he imagines is Merteuil's view of his attachment to Tourvel, but by a greater and dramatic irony he is sowing in Merteuil's mind the seed of a plan that she should win and remain faithful to one man (Danceny) in order to thwart the Vicomte, who will mistakenly believe that, being in love with him, she must inevitably return to him.

Valmont is being truly hoodwinked by Merteuil with her feint of jealousy, and is ready to attribute the wrong motivation to her proposition in L.20. If he has concluded that her scheme for him to seduce Cécile is a means of getting him back in her clutches, or of deflecting him from an exclusive attachment to Tourvel of which she somehow had foreknowledge, he will see the bargain that the Marquise attempts to strike in L.20, however flippantly expressed, as an alternative ploy devised to enable her to get back her former lover at the earliest opportunity, taking account of his projects, and fail to understand that her underlying purpose is quickly to sever his ties with the Présidente so that he will then be free to perform her work of revenge. (Merteuil, for the moment, sees the seduction of the Présidente and of Cécile as opposed and incompatible plans.) In the second part of L.20, which deals with Cécile, Merteuil declares an interest in the girl and says that she is tempted to make her her pupil (in libertine studies, of course). On the surface Merteuil appears to have abandoned her original plan to have Valmont seduce Cécile (L.2), but her real intention is to provoke Valmont to take a proprietary interest in the girl and to want to rival the Marquise in "educating" her, demonstrating his skill where Danceny fails (for 'ce Danceny est un enfant qui perdra son temps à faire l'amour, et ne finira rien'—L.5, F43). Valmont may realise this but still discount the idea that Merteuil is serious in her wish for revenge on Gercourt, seeing it rather as the (old ?) stratagem of sidetracking him from the Présidente by getting him interested in Cécile. Thus, wrongly assuming Merteuil's persistent passion for him, he can foolishly discount both her bargain and her provocative plan to educate Cécile herself as the flexible tactics of a jealous woman, not realising that the very fact that Merteuil is trying a two-handed approach is a sign of her determination that Cécile must be corrupted and vengeance on Gercourt assured.

If Valmont intends to take his time with Tourvel (L.23) even though Merteuil has trailed tempting bait on a double hook before his eyes (L.20), then how is she to gain her revenge on Gercourt, given that Danceny 'ne finira rien' (L.5) ? If she puts insurmountable obstacles in the path of the Valmont-Présidente relationship by stiffening Tourvel's resistance, an affair with the unresisting Cécile will begin to seem to him an attractive proposition by contrast. Nothing will be more welcome than light relief and a facile interlude in the pursuit of the 'grande passion', and if the latter has to be abandoned he will need some woman of easy virtue with whom to salvage his wounded vanity, and who better for all concerned than Cécile ? Mention of the 'secrets' that Merteuil tells Cécile's mother (L.31) is a strong hint that the Marquise is strengthening Mme de Volanges's warnings to the Présidente against Valmont, and L.32 bears all the hallmarks of Merteuil's influence.[9]

Valmont, of course, knows nothing of the machinations behind L.32—despite his later discovery (L.44) of Mme de Volanges's letters against him—for there is no way he can recognise the evidence of Merteuil's treachery in them. Even supposing he did know of the Marquise's attempt to frustrate his affair, he would interpret it as proof of her passionate jealousy of Tourvel. For Merteuil never says anything to dispel the illusion of her covert love for him. After her secret talk with Mme de Volanges she can afford, in L.33, to criticise Valmont's seduction techniques, no doubt because she thinks that his bid to win the Présidente through letters will fail, not only for the reasons she states in that letter but because Tourvel, through her efforts, now has a moral mentor whose advice, Merteuil assumes, will not be gainsaid. Her phrase 'il n'y a rien de si difficile en amour, que d'écrire ce qu'on ne sent pas' (L.33, F100) seems to acknowledge that Valmont is not in love with the Présidente (cp. L.10)—she can permit herself to defer this much to his libertine image as a cold ruthless seducer (see L.23, F81) now that she has taken steps to thwart his affair. That Merteuil should apparently be retreating from complaints (in his view essentially motivated by jealousy) that he was in love with Tourvel does not, however, induce him to reassess his view of the Marquise, for that phrase 'il n'y a rien de si difficile, etc.', beneath the whole tone of libertine badinage in L.33, very indirectly insinuates—unless this is to push the interpretation too far—that she perhaps thinks his real attachment is to herself and not to Tourvel: the sort of self-deception only a passionate woman would be capable of.

Nevertheless, despite Merteuil's careful planning, Mme de Volanges's warnings go unheeded, while the Marquise concludes that the cause of revenge is best served by presenting Valmont with the choice of the two women in the same locale. As for Valmont, there is nothing in Merteuil's letters to disabuse him of that delusion concerning her real feelings for him which is established once he thinks he has detected jealousy and spotted a face-saving plan to welcome him back as her lover. Confident of his irresistibility to all women (including former partners), why should he not think that when Merteuil pimps for Cécile (L.38, F113, and L.54, F151) she hopes that his vanity will lead him to supplant the inadequate Danceny who is 'si Céladon' (L.51), and that in this the rancour she harbours against Gercourt is subservient to her desire to deflect him from the Présidente by presenting Cécile as the lure ? L.66 has Valmont paying lip service to what he imagines is Merteuil's over-strident and perhaps feigned obsession with revenge through the medium of Danceny (their plans have now coincided—see L.44), but also envisaging the failure of these plans through a scandal which would prevent the Gercourt marriage; if Valmont wants the strength of her reaction to the possibility of failure to be a test of credibility, she does not respond. The tone of *hauteur* with which Merteuil announces that it is she who has set up the options of love and revenge for Valmont (L.74 and L.85) does not point, he must think, to her indifference about his designs on Tourvel, but conceals the irritation of a woman who is forcing herself to cooperate in his seduction of the Présidente so as to get the whole episode over with, for only then can she hold her old lover to the terms of the agreement in L.20, only then will Valmont return to her arms.

(In reality the Marquise must be secretly congratulating herself on a skilful move to ensure that if Danceny lacks initiative, then Valmont will be more enterprising with Cécile.) Nor can the Vicomte believe that Merteuil's vaunted libertinism is anything more than a superficial image which he can take at face value only when it is to his advantage to do so.

No doubt as he sees it, she conceived of the separation pact ('nous séparant pour le bonheur du monde', F39) because she unwillingly bowed to the inevitable (Valmont's infidelity) and dressed it up as a 'mission d'amour' (*ibid*.), becoming a pseudo-male libertine herself out of spite at his incapacity for constancy. He cannot accept L.81's analysis of Merteuil's intentional *libertinage* , consciously cultivated since her childhood: the Marquise's outburst in that letter involves a grossly exaggerated level of self-confidence. A gloating description of Valmont ogling the Présidente on his return to Mme de Rosemonde's château (L.76) has, he can surmise, found its mark. Merteuil's account of the beginning of her relationship with the Vicomte (L.81, F228) hardly corresponds with what he remembers, for did she not really interest herself in him at first because she had been abandoned by Gercourt ? And is not a capacity for emotional over-investment an unchanging part of her character ? If there is one distortion in L.81, then perhaps the whole letter is a distortion. As it appears to the Vicomte, her inflated self-esteem betrays the dent in her self-confidence as an attactive woman that his preference for Mme de Tourvel has made, and jealousy has been converted into anger and a determination to prove her greater sexually manipulative skills; the spirit of rivalry should be dispelled at the first convincing tenderness from him—but that can wait. Valmont will ignore only at his peril her warning that their rivalry is in earnest, that he has an opponent of at least equal strength (her success with Prévan—a riposte to the Vressac episode— demonstrates that fact, and not her jealousy of Tourvel), and that he can expect no quarter from her, nor any sign of genuine emotional weakness.

By L.106, Valmont comes to recognise that Merteuil is indeed serious about her revenge when he sees the lengths to which she is prepared to go to bring it about that Gercourt and nobody else marries a Cécile who shall be well and truly corrupted, but the Vicomte does not pause to revise retrospectively his view of the Marquise's motivation earlier. He does not stop to reconsider whether the pique Merteuil showed at the beginning of the book was not caused by his initial refusal to be the instrument of her vengeance rather than any feeling of jealousy, or whether jealousy has not been simulated for private purposes. Long-standing preconceptions are hard to remove and he cannot but believe that she is secretly in love with him, for shortly afterwards she names Danceny as her new lover. To Valmont this looks like an attempt to force him either to make his top priority not the seduction of Tourvel but preventing Merteuil from seducing Danceny, or at least to speed up the affair with Tourvel so that he can claim his reward (L.20) and forestall the installation of an unsuitable replacement for Belleroche.

At the end of L.113, Merteuil asks Valmont to restrain Danceny from meeting Cécile—precisely the reverse of her original idea (see L.63, F170-71). Valmont has obliged the Marquise (L.110, F320-322), yet apparently it is Danceny who is to be rewarded! (F331) The more she appreciates Danceny, the more she thinks ill of Cécile (L.106, F307-8), and already in L.105 it seems she has personal reasons for urging the girl to keep her sentimental lover at arm's length which are quite distinct from those jesuitical hypocrisies with which she plies the young Volanges (F303-304) so as to break down her resistance to Valmont. Clearly her manoeuvres to retaliate against Gercourt through Valmont and her plans for the promotion of Danceny to the status of *Chevalier régnant* are conceived simultaneously and are complementary parts of a single strategy.

No sooner has Merteuil observed her revenge to be at last in sight (on receiving Valmont's report of his "debauchery" of Cécile, L.110, following instructions, L.106) than she proclaims Danceny as her new lover (L.113). Perhaps she considers that the setback of L.100 will provide just the sort of obstacle to provoke Valmont into making an unstinted effort to seduce the Présidente, but by announcing her choice of Danceny as the next in line to Belleroche she is signalling her refusal to ratify the terms of the contract of L.20 in the likely event of the Vicomte's success. It is logical to assume that Merteuil only made the bargain of L.20 in order to free Valmont from the trammels of Tourvel for the work of revenge, and not to win back her former partner by hook or by crook, if when she achieves her revenge by other means (by arranging for the Vicomte to carry on a double seduction) she immediately declines—by implication—to abide by the earlier agreement. Valmont himself must think that Merteuil only made the arrangement of L.20 as a desperate ploy to revive their former relationship in the long term; his whole treatment of her in the letters from L.125 onwards has to be interpreted as based on the assumption that he is dealing with a passionate woman, and his misconception apparently remains unshaken. That being so, he must credit the Marquise with merely using Danceny as a provocation, thinking that her selection of the young man as a witty and sensitive substitute for a 'Manœuvre d'amour' (F330) is a sign of her impatience with his never-ending pursuit of Tourvel (cf. the final words in L.106 'Pour ce qui est de moi [...] vous voyez bien qu'il faut encore attendre; et vous conviendrez, sans doute, que ce n'est pas ma faute'). The charming Danceny she describes (F331) is so far removed from the naive and gullible young man he knows (L.96, F269) that he cannot concede that she might literally follow his earlier suggestion ('Ou reprenez-moi, ou au moins prenez-en un autre', L.15, F63) in this case, and is not just employing the threat of seducing Danceny as a lever against him. If he thought there was something more than a lover's provocation in this, it is unlikely he would openly tell the Marquise that he was thwarting her plans by furthering the Cécile-Danceny affair (L.115, F337-8). It is a flattering notion to his ego that all she really wants is more attention from him.

For her part, Merteuil on the one hand may well be convinced that Valmont will not get the Présidente to capitulate for some time: she, Merteuil, has arranged that Cécile will return to Valmont, thus procuring something of a diversion (L.106). The Marquise knows she cannot immediately have Danceny, for she must go to the country to see to the lawsuit and to get rid of Belleroche. Does she then announce Danceny as her next lover, at a point at which she knows she cannot pursue to completion her plans for him, in order to put herself in competition with Valmont with an equal handicap ? For the Présidente has fled to Paris away from Valmont just as she must leave Paris and Danceny for the country. It seems almost like a challenge she has set herself to prove that she will be able to seduce Danceny more quickly and skilfully than Valmont can the Présidente. On the other hand, she may think Valmont will be inspired by sheer frustration (see L.100) to seduce [l'] *ingrate Dévote* in the not too distant future, particularly since poor health as a result of his over-indulgence with Cécile, the effects on the impressionable Tourvel of the reporting of this (F322-3), and boredom with the young Volanges who lacks the quality of sensibility he so admires in Tourvel, give him a motive for leaving Mme de Rosemonde's château to return to Paris and the Présidente. In that case, to say that she has set her sights on Danceny is to tell the Vicomte openly that he will not get his reward from her for a successful conclusion to his libertine campaign against Mme de Tourvel, knowing that he will not take her seriously. Merteuil is bluffing him by telling him the literal truth, a technique first apparent in L.20, F72: 'Quelle est donc en effet l'insolente sécurité de cet homme, qui ose dormir tranquille, tandis qu'une femme, qui a à se plaindre de lui, ne s'est pas encore vengée ?'

*****

Given Valmont's view of Merteuil as a woman with a secret passion for him which belies the libertine self-image of L.81, how are we to interpret his tactics in letters 125 to 144 ?

L.125 is the initial puzzle we are faced with, and particularly the effect—if any is consciously intended—which the end of the letter, in Valmont's estimation, will have on Merteuil. Are the sensations which Valmont experiences when Mme de Tourvel accepts his advances willingly for the first time to be taken as nothing more than 'la douce impression du sentiment de la gloire' (F358) masquerading as love ? [10] It is noteworthy that the words 'L'ivresse fut complète et réciproque; et, pour la première fois, la mienne survécut au plaisir. Je ne sortis de ses bras que pour tomber à ses genoux, pour lui jurer un amour éternel; et, il faut tout avouer, je pensais ce que je disais' follow immediately upon the Présidente's confession:

> je ne puis plus supporter mon existence, qu'autant qu'elle servira à vous rendre heureux. Je m'y consacre tout entière: dès ce moment je me donne à vous... (F366)

Arguably Valmont's responses have nothing to do with love, nor are they the sign of genuine emotional involvement with a woman who has touched in him a hitherto buried capacity for sensibility; this is no more than the glorified feeling of gratitude that the Présidente has fulfilled his wishes, the ego satisfaction that his plan—'Ce n'est pas assez pour moi de la posséder, je veux qu'elle se livre' (L.110, F320: cp. 'Pour que je sois vraiment heureux, il faut qu'elle se donne', L.6, F46)—has finally come to fruition. If Valmont thinks he is presenting the triumph of the will even at the emotional high point of his encounter with Tourvel, then this accounts for his surprise at L.127, and it might also explain how he can think that compliments to Merteuil such as calling her 'la véritable souveraine de [son] cœur' (L.129, F375) are not incongruous in the context of this description. But Valmont's bewilderment at the beginning of L.129 is artificial. Merteuil's reaction in L.127 was what he expected (he cannot see that she is *suspiciously* willing to oblige with the correct hint of passionate jealousy, to be taken as lurking behind the affront to her self-respect as a libertine which, she seems to say, his putting her in third place after Tourvel *and Cécile* has caused her). For his letter 125 portrays a unique emotional experience with a rival and projects it at a woman he takes to be jealous. The feelings evoked in Valmont in the crucial encounter with the Présidente are not necessarily to be regarded as a direct consequence of Mme de Tourvel's words quoted above. Clearly Valmont's intention at the end of L.125 is to pinpoint a quite exceptional moment of tenderness and personal commitment which transcends any feeling of self-congratulation on a successful seduction, and to juxtapose this in a cruel and insulting way with a request to Merteuil for bed and for his reward as agreed. This is not a failure of sensitivity, or a failure, out of hubris, to find the correct tone, or a misapprehension that Merteuil as a libertine will not be shocked: it is a deliberate insult aimed at a woman who, he thinks, cannot openly protest without revealing too much that contradicts her libertine image.

The clue to reading the letter as a provocation is Valmont's quoting of an old love letter of his to Merteuil ('*Oui, adieu, mon Ange! Je t'envoie tous les baisers de l'amour* '), just a few lines after telling her that 'L'ivresse fut complète et réciproque; et, pour la première fois, la mienne survécut au plaisir' (F366);[11] 'apparemment' in the sentence near the beginning of L.129 may be a revealing detail, too: 'Quel est donc ce crime que j'ai commis, *apparemment* sans m'en douter, et qui

94

vous donne tant d'humeur?' (F373, my italics). Thus Valmont responds to the provocation of L.113 with a counter-provocation in L.125: if the Marquise wants to choose Danceny as a new lover—a man she cannot be in love with if, as Valmont wrongly thinks, she still harbours a secret passion for him—then the Vicomte will demand casual infidelities to Tourvel with Merteuil—a woman he cannot possibly love given his unique experience with 'l'adorable femme' (F365). What has Valmont to lose by insulting the Marquise if she remains a soft touch ? He can save his reward for later when an opportune moment arises to "prove" his preference for her. For there are many ways in which to work on Merteuil—the ambivalent compliment, the subtle apology playing upon her libertine image, the dropping of further hints of his love for Tourvel or producing unreliable denials of it. Can he not manipulate her into unequivocally demanding what she will now consider the impossible sacrifice of Tourvel, thereby exposing her emotional dependence on him and enabling him by a conspicuous desertion to prove satisfactorily to himself that he is not enslaved to any individual woman, not even to such an incomparable one as the Présidente ? But the duper, deluding himself in thinking he can win control of his own feelings and of Merteuil too, soon becomes the duped.

Letters 125 to 145 are to my mind the most difficult part of the book and well-nigh impenetrable as far as ascribing motivation and understanding strategy goes. True, it is not difficult to determine the objectives of Merteuil. With her revenge on Gercourt at last in sight despite delays (L.111), she can turn her attention now to punishing Valmont for his various refusals to obey or to oblige, and for his insulting self-confidence. Merteuil is capable of harbouring grievances for a long time (as her long-delayed revenge on Gercourt proves): Valmont will inevitably have to pay for his initial refusal to seduce Cécile, and the Marquise's decision to stand by Danceny and refuse

Valmont his reward is a response to this and to other acts of disobedience no less than it is a reaction to the end of L.125. For Valmont is not the most obliging of men: he lets nine letters go by before mentioning the bargain of L.20; he will not consent to tell the story of Prévan's 'triple aventure' on cue; his reaction to her success with Prévan (L.96) is belated and grudging, maladroit, even (v. the post-scriptum to L.125).

Nor is the actual outcome of events in any way problematical: by believing in Mertueil's pretence of love for him, Valmont is manipulated through his vanity into sacrificing Tourvel without getting his reward. Inveigled into a spurious demonstration of mutually exclusive claims, he fails to prove his libertine freedom or his love for Merteuil, while giving the Marquise every incentive to put her plans for Danceny into action.

But what of Valmont and of his efforts to control events and influence his ex-partner ? Because he is wrapped up in an affair with his long-pursued conquest, and is responding passively to different stimuli, Valmont lacks the single-mindedness of his chief adversary: he may be suffering from a confusion of incompatible objectives. As usual, he wants to have his cake and eat it. Emotionally, he wants to keep Tourvel; intellectually, he needs to break with her to prove his freedom. He wants to hurt and worry Merteuil, but he aims also to win his reward from her. The tactics employed to that end are sometimes obscure: does he use bogus argument because he thinks that Merteuil, blinded by passion, will find it convincing ? Is he himself not even aware of how unconvincing he sounds ? Does he want Merteuil to find his arguments unreliable so that she will set him a test of his love for her, by responding to which he can wipe out all traces of the insult of L.125 and win his reward ? It seems he intends to get his reward from Merteuil, if possible without breaking with Tourvel, if necessary through sacrificing her.

One point stands out: it is inconceivable that Valmont would have made the unilateral sacrifice of Tourvel unless he thought it an effective way of winning his reward from the woman he took to be in love with him. Letters 125 to 145, which open with the Vicomte's triumph, chronicle his defeat at the hands of the only woman who declines to become his victim; he gambles on winning self-respect and his reward by abandoning his only real love, and he loses all; this is the first stage in the finally fatal breakdown of relations between the two protagonists, which ends in a mutual revenge whose fruits neither party is in any position to savour. Valmont's confidence that he can simultaneously manage, capitalise, even, on the two sides to Merteuil's private persona—the libertine and the secret lover—turns out to be misplaced; the Marquise is the "simple" libertine she always said she was, and she can bluff and blind him with hints of the truth alongside a feint of romantic nostalgia and yearning.

*****

At first sight there seems much to be said for the idea that Valmont thinks of Merteuil as no more than a careless libertine, a sexual realist with no time for sentimentality and with no buried emotional weaknesses—not least if this will simplify the interpretation of Valmont's actions and statements in this section of letters (Ll.125 ff.). Perhaps, after all, he does see her plan in L.20, not as a recherché scheme to win back her old lover while saving face, but as a malicious *jeu d'esprit* in the fulfilment of which Merteuil must nevertheless be held to her word. He talks in L.76 (F199) of 'les mille et mille caprices qui gouvernent la tête d'une femme, et *par qui seuls* vous tenez encore à votre sexe' (my italics), so does he not perhaps subscribe himself to the superior view she takes of herself (L.81) ? Would he really expect Merteuil to advise him on how to 'hâter [sa] marche' and win Tourvel if he thought the Marquise secretly loved him (L.100) ? At the end of L.115, he says 'vous posséder et vous perdre, c'est acheter un moment de bonheur par une éternité de regrets' (F338), implying that Merteuil has a "love-them-and-leave-them" attitude towards her lovers. Moreover, does he *not* guard against linking the evidence of his love for Tourvel with a request for his reward from Merteuil (L.57 and L.125) precisely because he thinks that she, as a libertine, stands above jealousy ?

If all this sounds feasible, then perhaps Valmont's view of Merteuil's attitudes and reactions in L.127-141 is something like this: here is a "woman of the head", he thinks, who is obtusely demanding as the price of his reward that he accord her the same emotional treatment and courting, pledges and proofs, as he would a "woman of the heart". Very well, he will pander to her whim, and pretend not to notice that her demands break the libertine code and amount to a request for a pseudo-marital loving and devotedly faithful relationship. But at the same time as he humours her in this charade, he will make it perfectly plain what his real attitude to her is. Hence he talks of the 'marche franche et libre' of his approach in L.125, and of the value he attaches to it because it reminds him of the clear-eyed (sexual) happiness of the past, and shows that he prizes her for her capacity for sexual response (mentioning the 'délicieux plaisirs qu'[elle] seule [sait] rendre toujours nouveaux, comme toujours plus vifs') while simultaneously calling her 'la véritable souveraine de [son] cœur' (L.129, F373-5) ! Hence he perhaps insinuates that she is only interested in how good he is in bed, or in his reputation (L.133, F383), while going along with her anti-libertine request for an almost marital relationship with him ('Oui, sans doute, vous me fixerez', F385). Any pretence of jealousy which she might summon up would be countered with an equally factitious denial that he is emotionally involved with Tourvel (v. 'de ce que l'esprit est occupé, s'ensuit-il que le cœur soit esclave?', F384—unless this is a piece of self-persuasion), and a shower of compliments which seem as much addressed to a sensualist as to a sentimental woman (F385). Hence, also, he does not respond to L.134 with an immediate sacrifice of Tourvel, and the denial of his love for Tourvel issued at the beginning of L.138 is allowed to sound unreliable, perhaps because he is not convinced that Merteuil genuinely resents his interest in the Présidente. Hence, after proving his love for Merteuil by sacrificing Tourvel (v. L.142, F406: 'Je suis curieux, surtout, de savoir si, dans cette dernière démarche, vous trouverez encore de l'amour. Ah! sans doute, il y en a, et beaucoup! Mais pour qui ?')—for this is all part of the 'insipide cajolerie' (L.129) which the Marquise pretends to need—he makes it clear that he wants his reward from the libertine he knew of old whom he invites to come back to Paris to 'retrouver votre Amant, vos plaisirs, vos amis, *et le courant des aventures* ' (L.144, F409, my italics). This version of Valmont's view of things at least has the merit of explaining some of the sudden reversals and contradictions in Valmont's arguments in this difficult section of letters (Ll.125 ff.).

Unfortunately, if it does not stand up to close scrutiny, we must return to our original line of attack in order to offer some possible explanations of Valmont's ambiguous approach and tactics and his inconsistency:

(i) Of course the Vicomte can afford to pay lip service to Merteuil's libertine image in contexts where it suits his argument to do so, or as a part of some ironic excuse for thwarting plans of hers which he does not take seriously (L.115); that does not mean he thinks her libertinism is the whole story.

(ii) As regards L.100, while enjoying torturing Merteuil, the woman he takes to love him still, with the sight of his interest in Tourvel rapidly turning into an authentic 'hantise d'amour', Valmont is quite capable of assuming that, her secret love notwithstanding, she will nevertheless help him in his affair with a rival, so that having won her and with desire sated, his disenchanted recognition of Tourvel as a 'femme ordinaire' (L.96, F268) will bring back to his mind an appreciation of Merteuil's more substantial qualities. Has she not already provided him with cover, enabling him to return to Mme de Rosemonde's château ?

(iii) For what reason is the strongest evidence of Valmont's love for Tourvel always deliberately juxtaposed by him with a demand for bed and for his reward from the Marquise ? Obviously this is intended as an insult (L.57 and L.125). He can only presume it is an insult if he presumes Merteuil really does secretly love him, so what is it that makes him change his mind and decide thereafter that she is just obtusely demanding that she be treated as if she did ? (Nothing on this is to be found in the text; nor does he change his mind.)

(iv) Unless it is the case that Valmont miscalculates in thinking that because Merteuil loves him the sacrifice of Tourvel will win him his reward, then Merteuil's triumphant claims to have duped him (L.145) are spurious. Yet to the reader this is surely one of the most convincing letters in the book. The part of her remarks most relevant to our discussion is this:

> Où en seriez-vous à présent, si je n'avais voulu que vous faire une malice ? Mais je suis incapable de tromper, vous le savez bien; et dussiez-vous, à mon tour, me réduire au désespoir et au Couvent, j'en cours les risques, et je me rends à mon vainqueur. (L.145, F411)

The irony of these words turns upon the point that Merteuil is *not* the victim of her love for Valmont, like Tourvel, but Valmont's conqueror, whom she has deluded with her feint of love for him, whom she has ensnared into making a sacrifice which will go unrewarded. The chief meaning of 'vous faire une malice' is 'getting you to sacrifice Tourvel without giving myself to you in return', but in the particular and general contexts it includes the idea of achieving that end by exploiting his vanity and by a pretence of feeling. In retrospect the answer to the (originally rhetorical) question 'qui de nous deux se chargera de tromper l'autre ?' (L.131, F379) turns out to be 'Merteuil'; 'je suis incapable de tromper, vous le savez bien' is an ironic reference back to that letter 131 where the Marquise first baited the tender traps with nostalgic yearning, and L.151 gives further weight to the irony. Valmont does not sacrifice Tourvel despite sensing that when Merteuil plays the role of a passionate woman it is all a pointless charade, but does so because he fails to see that this is all play-acting with a single purpose—to trick him. Out of a long-standing mistaken character assessment, he fails to distinguish the real person from the role. Valmont loses Tourvel for being unconvincing about merely playing the part of her lover (Merteuil holds him to his word, and 'ce n'est pas ma faute si...' of L.138, F396 is ironically paralleled in the break-off letter in L.141, F404). Merteuil wins her revenge over him by being convincing in playing the role of his secret lover who gradually declares herself. Then in L.145 , the real woman speaks, and what she says comes as a bombshell to him.

*****

Let us now take a close look at Letters 127 to 144, chiefly from Valmont's viewpoint, in order to pinpoint uncertainties about his tactics and to examine not only the contradictions in which he is involved, but also the blind spots in his perception of the situation and what they may lead to in his mistaken approach towards bending Merteuil to do his will and grant him his reward.

The Vicomte's intentional insult to the Marquise in L.125—counting on her readiness to go to bed with him when he loves another—is no doubt meant as a rap over the knuckles for her threat of having Danceny as her lover (L.113). The first and very fundamental mistake he makes is to imagine that he can somehow neutralise the effect of L.125 upon Merteuil and win his reward from her later. For Merteuil is not in fact the secret lover whom he is directed to see gradually emerging from behind her libertine mask (L.131 and L.134), and who can be placated with some at any rate *ultimately* convincing demonstration of his more than merely sexual interest in her, but she is a strict libertine who judges Valmont to have broken the first rule in the libertine code that there must be no emotional involvement with the victim. There is absolutely no reason why she should agree to abide by the arrangement of L.20 (whether interpreted as an invitation to a one-night stand or to a more permanent affair) if she is convinced by his description of the 'ivresse [...] complète et réciproque' which for him 'pour la première fois [...] survécut au plaisir' (F366). Why should she ever give him his reward simply to help him prove to himself that he is capable of emotional *disponibilité* and that 'la faculté de [s'] en faire jouir [sc. de son bonheur] dans toute son énergie' is not 'réservée à telle ou telle femme, exclusivement à toute autre' ? (L.125, F358-9)

Merteuil's response to L.125 does not appear to be the reaction of someone who is jealous of one particular rival, but rather that of a woman whose self-respect is being jeopardised by his putting her last of three (L.127). Valmont must imagine that by bracketing Cécile and Tourvel together she is hiding her jealousy of Tourvel behind a general sense of outrage.[12] He only discovers later, from L.145, that Merteuil's desire for revenge on the Présidente was not motivated by passionate jealousy as such.

The consequent withholding of his reward means that Valmont must now move from insult to apology and to compliment if he seriously wishes to get it (L.129). Yet L.129 is a farrago of contradictions and implausible remarks, for using Merteuil's libertine image to explain away his attitude towards her at the end of L.125 makes it impossible for him to invent convincing compliments. At the start of L.129, Valmont compounds the injury of L.125 (end) by facile lying, which by denying the truth, simply draws attention to it:

> En réunissant l'espoir au désir, je n'ai fait que céder à l'impulsion naturelle, qui nous fait nous placer toujours le plus près possible du bonheur que nous cherchons; et vous avez pris pour l'effet de l'orgueil ce qui ne l'était que de mon empressement. (F373)

The rest of the letter is equally transparently dishonest—and inconsistent, moreover. Why should Merteuil consider herself 'la véritable souveraine de [son] cœur' (F375), given his qualification of Tourvel in L.100 as '[celle] qui fait le charme et le tourment de ma vie!' (F287) and given his account of the 'charme inconnu' and of an 'ivresse [qui] pour la première fois survécut au plaisir' (L.125) ? How can Merteuil monopolise his feelings in this way and be the only woman he prefers if she is only able to provide him with 'délicieux plaisirs' ? (F374) Why should he prefer the said 'délicieux plaisirs' with Merteuil if his heart is 'flétri' but for Tourvel's saving powers (L.6, F46) ? (For there can be no doubt that these pleasures are no more than sexual, in view of his memories of their former affair in the second paragraph of L.129.) When placed in the balance 'plaisirs [...] *toujours nouveaux* , [...] *toujours plus vifs* ' can never outweigh 'charme *inconnu* ' (my italics). Is not his end compliment ('véritable souveraine') an 'insipide cajolerie' (F373) in itself, and could it not be said to be merely a function of 'la situation dans laquelle on se trouve quand on en parle' (F374): i.e. Merteuil is a jealous woman demanding attention so he will soft-soap her? To contrast his 'marche franche et libre' (F373) in propositioning Merteuil in L.125 with 'insipide cajolerie' and then to finish off L.129 with a prize piece of 'cajolerie' which cannot be reconciled with his sketch of her purely sexual talents elsewhere in the letter might suggest that Valmont is not calculatedly indulging in inadequate argument: he simply *is* inadequate and lacking in persuasive power.

Is he unconvincing because he is not really concerned as yet to win his reward and because he cannot resist annoying Merteuil further with the very spuriousness of his remarks, in a letter which ironically cancels itself out on its own terms as well as in comparison with letters in its vicinity ? Is the business of apology and self-justification so demeaning to his ego that he can allow himself to construct for his private amusement a tissue of arguments that are self-consciously unconvincing, chauvinistically relying on Merteuil's supposed love-blindness and postulated wish, despite the insult of L.125, to win him back as her lover to make her satisfied with one or two hyperbolic endearments (and a mere hint of his readiness to prefer her to Tourvel) as the price of his reward ? Or does he think that, with Merteuil's aptitude for detecting what is bogus strengthened by her jealousy, she will explicitly set a test for him to prove she is 'la véritable souveraine de [son] cœur' ?—a test which, if he comes through with flying colours, will erase from her mind any suspicion that he is merely paying court to her to persuade himself that he is not 'maîtrisé comme un écolier, par un sentiment involontaire et inconnu' (F358). Are his unbelievable compliments part of an attempt to show how difficult would be the sacrifice of Tourvel first referred to in L.127 ? The more incredible his compliments to Merteuil and his denials of involvement with Tourvel become, the more impossible appears the sacrifice, and thus the more meritorious when it is finally made and the more effectual as a means of winning his reward—is *this* perhaps what he thinks ?

Letters 133 and 138 raise similar multiple possibilities of interpretation. In the former, does Valmont think that his assertion of no more than an intellectual interest in his experiment with Tourvel alongside the mere promise of a sacrifice is sufficient inducement for Merteuil to become amenable, [13] or does he expect her to discern a self-deception on his part which will lead her to insist that he validate in a concrete way the preference he expressed for her in L.129 ? Does he suppose that he can simultaneously play upon her libertine image and her feelings for him with such a dubious verification of his libertine credentials and such a feeble denial of his passion for Tourvel ? [14] Is he most concerned, in fact, with his own self-respect as a libertine and free spirit, and not even aware of deceiving himself with an inadequate proof of his emotional detachment from the Présidente ? In the latter (L.138), does he aim to get his 'récompense' (F366), without the need for an irrevocable desertion of Tourvel, by counting on Merteuil's love to permit her to accept his supposed proof that he is not in love with the Présidente if he can leave her for the night ? Or does he want her jealously to suspect that he cannot give up the woman permanently if he arranges a reconciliation ?—so that in consequence she will request in black and white that he abandon Tourvel for good, because he thinks he can outmanoeuvre the Marquise and extract his prize by doing something she had thought him incapable of. Is he self-deludedly justifying to himself his unwillingness to give up Tourvel as a tactic to enable him to manipulate Merteuil ? [15]

Whether (and for whatever reasons) the unreliability of Valmont's argument is calculated or unconscious, in either case he is wrong to assume that Merteuil loves him and will therefore compensate him. Ironically, Valmont may just possibly prefer to think that, by hinting at his indomitable love for Mme de Tourvel, he is manipulating Merteuil into demanding in clear-cut terms that he sacrifice her and thus he can win his reward, while the Marquise, by hinting at her love for him, is manipulating him into making the sacrifice so that she can refuse him it. There can be little doubt that such is her purpose in L.131.[16] She pretends to find his compliments at the end of L.129 acceptable, but capitalises on the point that Valmont only experiences sexual desire for her (as shown in his supposed preference for 'délicieux plaisirs' over 'charme inconnu') as far as to reject his offer to seek her out in her country house and establish something more than an ephemeral liaison with her (cf. 'mille fois et de mille manières', F375). She is prepared to grant him a one-night stand, to be put off until she returns to Paris, and for which a precondition would be her first winning Danceny (cf. 'une infidélité réciproque', F380); for love, not merely sexual desire, is needed as the basis of a long-term relationship, and 'de l'amour, en a-t-on quand on veut ?' (F378). In crude terms, Valmont interprets L.131 to mean that if he wants a durable renewal of their old affair (as his hyperbolic compliment in the penultimate paragraph of L.129 suggested) he will need to convince her that he feels for her something more lasting than sexual desire, and he will have to give up Tourvel and remain faithful to her. As a *pis-aller* , a one-off encounter (in the 'petite maison'?) is possible, but the price she is asking for that is permission to have Danceny first. Valmont sees Merteuil as now demanding the sentimental response to her that he accords to the Présidente: he may well feel that by equivocally playing upon her libertine image in L.129 he has trapped her into lifting the libertine mask, putting her cards on the table, and finally admitting that her attitude towards love, as far as he was concerned, was not the brutally realistic one of L.81. Valmont's mistake is to presume that she really does want a permanent liaison: by her nostalgia about the past, by her hint that she had loved him but he had deceived her, so that now she desires an arrangement of strict marital loving fidelity, he is fooled into thinking that he will win his reward if only he sacrifice Tourvel.[17] While it takes him till L.142 to break with the Présidente, L.131 lays the foundations of his misconception about the deal Merteuil is offering him.

Since Merteuil disdainfuly said of Belleroche in L.113 that 'Il me prise donc bien peu, s'il croit valoir assez pour me fixer!' (F330), Valmont ought to be on his guard when the libertine with pseudo-male values reverts to traditional roles, talks of being unsure of Valmont's capacity for fidelity ('et puis, comment vous fixer ?' F380), and mimics the attitudes of a sentimental woman (cp. 'fixer', F141) in order to entice him into sacrifices she has no intention of reciprocating.[18] But Merteuil's evocation of their old love comes as no surprise to him because he had always assumed that her libertinism was a mask to conceal emotional weakness: he does not, for instance, parry with an apposite quotation from L.81, such as 'l'amour que l'on nous vante comme la cause de nos plaisirs, n'en est au plus que le prétexte' (F225), because, of course, he had never believed L.81. Like the other characters he is ripe for manipulation, and Merteuil, in a sense, can bluff him with the truth. She mentions 'les conditions d'un marché qui vous intéresse *peut-être* moins que vous ne voulez me le faire croire' and asks him to 'différer un moment que je désire *peut-être* autant que vous' (F379; my italics): the two parallel 'peut-être' clearly indicate that neither of them has their heart in the wiping out of the old debt (L.20). Yet Valmont takes it that she would really prefer something rather more glamorous than a brief encounter, if only she could be sure of his ability to sacrifice Tourvel, reciprocate her own love, and tolerate a monogamous relationship. She declares 'D'abord, j'exigerais des sacrifices [...] qu'il se peut bien que je ne mérite pas' (F380), thus signalling her intention to keep Danceny, come what may, while forcing Valmont to surrender Tourvel. But the Vicomte cannot read the signs.

On the surface Valmont appears to react to L.131 as if he saw through Merteuil's nostalgia (L.133). When he apparently indirectly classifies her as a woman who is only interested in the quantity not the quality of his love-making, or in his reputation (F383), he seems to be indicating that he is not taken in by her pretence of nostalgia for a past when she supposedly loved him with her whole heart. The self-correction in the phrase at the end of L.133 'Ne combattez donc plus *l'idée, ou plutôt le sentiment* que vous ramène à moi' (F385, my italics) looks like nothing more than grudging lip service to her supposed feelings for him. His exhortation that she should return to him so that they can experience once against the 'délicieux [sexual] plaisirs' of the past seems precisely *not* the kind of argument he would use to entice a woman whose heart he believed really had been, and remains, engaged (*ibid* .). Is not his readiness to return Cécile to Danceny (F384-5) a sign that he takes seriously her threat to have Danceny (cf. 'une infidélité réciproque', F380), and does not believe that she really would like to resurrect their old affair; and will not his suspicions be increased by her refusal of his sacrifice of Cécile (L.134, F388) which is obviously intended to give her time to seduce 'le jeune homme'? (F331).

But if the reason why Valmont only talks of sacrificing Tourvel (L.133) or only sacrifices her temporarily (L.138) is that he realises Merteuil is determined to get Danceny and is only playing on her supposed feelings (L.131 and L.134) in order to force him to make a one-sided sacrifice of Tourvel, then the reader finds it totally incomprehensible that he should make the sacrifice nevertheless, even granted the importance to his self-respect of his maintaining his libertine image. For his will to outmanoeuvre Merteuil is bound up with his libertine pride no less than is his desire to discredit his love for Tourvel, and, in the circumstances, would be the more important concern. The mistake Valmont makes is to discount Danceny and to take it for granted that the sacrifice of Tourvel will win him his reward because the Marquise loves him as she did in the past and wants him to come back to her for good. The arguments of L.133 are based, then, on the postulation that Merteuil does indeed feel for him: they are in response to the end of L.131 which was, to the deluded Valmont, a revelation of what he had always suspected to be the truth. If, therefore, Valmont appears to treat the Marquise as if he believed her to be a thorough-going libertine, then this must be no more than a *feint* of disbelief in the sentiments she had expressed at the end of L.131, which is designed to extract a more explicit confession of her love. The contrivance of one libertine talking to another about his "experiment" is useful, for he can avoid having to respond to Merteuil's indirect declaration with some endearment or pledge of mutual love which suggests he is enslaved to her: for the sake of his libertine image he needs to repudiate the notion that he is enslaved to *any* woman. In any case he cannot openly talk of love yet, so soon after ironically quoting an old love letter in the context of his feelings for another woman (F366).

It has to be said that, behind all the ambiguities, the hard linguistic evidence on which can be based the proposition that Valmont believes he is addressing a libertine whose nostalgia in L.131 is counterfeit is slight indeed '...vous doutez de mes sentiments *ou de mon énergie* ?' (F382, my italics) seems like a significant correction from one libertine to another, but 'énergie' in this context amounts to an indication of Valmont's determination not to be passively trapped in an emotional affair with the Présidente, and is thus not necessarily in a totally different category from 'mes sentiments'. The derogatory allocation of Merteuil to one of two classes of insensitive women who are uninterested in feelings is an inducement to the Marquise to show her feelings more clearly, or is more apparent than real, for Valmont does not specifically include all women but Tourvel in one section or the other.[19] The compliments in the last two paragraphs but one of L.133, with their talk of 'nos sentiments [...] restés unis' (F385), are a kind of mulish compromise between his former insistence on 'délicieux plaisirs' (L.129) and her more sentimental view of the past (L.131,

109

end). The correction 'l'idée, ou plutôt le sentiment qui vous ramène à moi' (F385) is not necessarily critical: this could be merely a reference back to the end of her previous letter ('Oh! non, non, je ne veux seulement pas m'occuper de cette idée', F380; cf. 'Une simple idée qui me vient', L.134, F386, and contrast V1369, n. 4, ref. to V311).

L.133 is addressed to a woman Valmont thinks loves him, not to one he realises is pretending to love him. Of the two options in settlement of the old debt (L.20) held out by Merteuil in L.131 (fourth paragraph and last paragraph) Valmont chooses the latter, emphasising 'l'espoir si doux que m'a donné votre Lettre', and assuring her 'Oui, sans doute, vous me fixerez' (F385), because he thinks it is the only option Merteuil is serious about. He could, though, with good grace, have found the first, with its provision for an 'infidélité réciproque', an acceptable compromise between Merteuil's choice of Danceny as her new lover (L.113) and his own request for his reward (end of L.125). He offers to give back Cécile to Danceny (F384) because he fancies that Merteuil is interested in him not in Danceny, and because he wishes to disprove any special attachment to the girl 'à laquelle [...] je tiens si peu' (*ibid* .) so that the Marquise can have no cause for complaint (see L.127). If Valmont really did treat seriously Merteuil's threat to have Danceny he would not simply talk of returning the girl to her young lover, he would make practical arrangements to see that it was done, since at that stage it is particularly important that Danceny, not the Vicomte, should take the blame for Cécile's pregnancy. No doubt he has made the assumption that a one-night stand involving an 'infidélité réciproque' is just a *pis-aller* to Merteuil, who is really angling in L.131 for a permanent relationship with him; he can therefore surrender Cécile to Danceny whenever he wants, without there being any danger of Merteuil's having run off with his alibi. The construction of an elaborate argument (F383-4) disavowing his love for Tourvel is aimed at a woman he imagines to have a passionate interest in finding it acceptable (or inadequate ?).

Merteuil is duly unimpressed by his account of his 'observation' (F383) of Tourvel, who, it appears, has some qualities which the Marquise has (until recently ?) sadly lacked:

> Enfin, il fallait qu'elle réunît encore cette candeur naturelle, devenue insurmontable par l'habitude de s'y livrer, et qui ne lui permet de dissimuler aucun des sentiments de son cœur. (F384)

(Here the movement from the subjunctive to the indicative illustrates an illusion of planning overtaken by fascination with the actual object of desire.) L.134 makes a little more explicit what the end of L.131 had hinted at: if the Vicomte by some conclusive act substantiates his allegation that he is not the self-deluded idolater of the Présidente, he will win his reward from Merteuil. Valmont's failure to respond with a genuine sacrifice (L.138), his temporary break with Mme de Tourvel soon followed by a reconciliation, is a sign of the struggle between his libertine conscience and his love for this 'femme délicate et sensible' (F384), but not an indicator of his suspicions about Merteuil's designs on Danceny and of his wish to keep Tourvel as a bargaining counter in a projected trade-off of partners. Thus Valmont misinterprets L.134, not understanding the significance of being allowed to keep Cécile for the moment, and not seeing that the options of L.131 have been subtly changed, so that while appearing to desire a full-blooded renewal of her liaison with him, Merteuil has no intention of renouncing her pursuit of Danceny. How precisely does the Vicomte come to be deceived ?

Valmont's lack of real surprise at Merteuil's covert declaration at the end of L.131 and his willingness to rise to the lure of 'sacrifices' no doubt suggest to her that despite having an emotional touchstone in the person of the Présidente, so convinced is he of his own irresistibility that he does not possess the critical discrimination to be able to spot the difference between emotional role-playing for a strategic advantage and the expression of a genuine attachment and longing, or is too concerned with his libertine image to see beyond his nose. In L.134, therefore, Mme de Merteuil can make signals, knowing that, most probably out of a distorted sense of his sentimental importance to her, he will fail to read them correctly: she can bluff him with hints of the truth alongside a pretence of affection in a confidential tone. Basing her position on Valmont's choice of the second option of L.131 and on his gambler's fascination with sacrifices, she reacts to L.133 precisely in the way that a passionate woman would be expected to: she refuses to accept him back as her lover unless he shows that actions speak louder than words and renounces his love for Tourvel and his over-idealised view of her.[20] The tokens of the Marquise's feeling for him come so thick and fast that in their context Valmont does not stop to consider the reasons for her insistence on his staying with Cécile for the time being, or finds a perfectly innocent explanation for it. For she ensnares him in a whole web of allusions to her love and her susceptibility.

Let us illustrate this last point. 'Tout simplement votre cœur abuse votre esprit, et le fait se payer de mauvaises raisons: mais moi, *qui ai un grand intérêt à ne pas m'y tromper* , je ne suis pas si facile à contenter' (F386-7; my italics) is clearly projected as the reasoning of a possessive lover. Yet she is determined, she says, not to react with irritation to the evidence of his love for Tourvel. To do so would be a 'piège dangereux' (F387), because, she implies, her previous annoyance at his interest in other women (L.127) led to a placatory offer from Valmont which she found dangerously enticing.[21] In the same way she lets it be understood that she finds the idea of his returning to her irresistible: 'Loin de me fâcher de vos refus, je vous en remercierai. Tenez, ce n'est pas avec vous que je veux dissimuler [cp. 'cette candeur naturelle etc.', F384], j'en ai peut-être besoin' (F387). She needs him to refuse to make the crucial sacrifice, because she cannot herself control her desire to have him back. 'Croyez-moi, ne soyons qu'amis, et restons-en là' (*ibid* .) mimics the authentic self-defensive voice of passion (cp. L.67, F180) with an irony which Valmont is too unobservant to notice.

Valmont must surmise from all this that Merteuil is so in love with him that she cannot recognise what a nonsense is the idea of his *wilfully* changing his attitude to Tourvel (instead of concluding that she cannot know what love is if she thinks it controllable by the will—F387-8). Is not Merteuil generous indeed, therefore, in permitting him temporary use of Cécile, so as to compensate for his implied desertion (as well as his new view) of the Présidente, when previously she had supposedly found his connection with the young Volanges so objectionable (L.127) that he had felt obliged to prove his indifference to the girl by offering to return her to her young lover (L.133) ? Valmont is being invited to think (first new paragraph, F388) that Merteuil, who has now omitted all reference to Cécile from the list of revealing adjectives (compare F387 and F370), is now admitting she is not passionately jealous of his relationship with the girl who has no emotional hold over him, and for whom he feels nothing that is the basis of a long-term liaison (cf. L.131)—only of Tourvel and her influence. [22] This confirms his impression that L.127 was a cover-up (*v. supra* , p. 102). With so many proofs of her passion emerging and dropping into place as expected, elicited by his playing the libertine card in L.133, he can have no inkling that Merteuil's purpose is really to make him a catspaw in her seduction of Danceny by, in effect, inducing him to keep the young lovers apart.[23]

Impressed by the rather exoteric cryptology of her love which Merteuil introduces into L.134, Valmont has mistakenly imposed a one-sided interpretation on that letter. But for those who can read again between the lines the letter does contain clues to Merteuil's real attitude and resolve that are much less obvious than is the evidence of her scheme to force the Vicomte to cooperate unknowingly in the waylaying of Danceny. For instance in the innocent-looking phrase 'tous les mots que *vous vous êtes imaginé* m'avoir déplu' (F387; my italics) Merteuil can afford to indicate her lack of real jealousy, knowing that she will not be believed—it is ironic that Valmont, who uses a similar tactic with the Présidente in L.68, cannot recognise the truth being presented as a bluff. She can permit herself, too, to analyse so perspicaciously the subjective delusion of the lover (F387-8), knowing he will not see that it undermines the foundations of her supposed love for him no less than of his for Tourvel. She can blind him with the truth by arguing that he is incapable of sacrificing the Présidente through a hypothesis which she intends to ensure will turn out to be true: 'puisque vous ne l'aviez jamais trouvé jusque-là [sc. 'ce charme inconnu'], il est bien à croire que vous ne le trouveriez pas davantage à l'avenir, et la perte que vous feriez n'en serait pas moins irréparable' (F387). With 'j'en ai peut-être besoin [sc. 'de vos refus']' (*ibid*.), she can hint at her love and manipulate him to take advantage of her "weakness", but by a private irony quietly think 'Yes, I need you to refuse to sacrifice Tourvel, because I certainly do not intend to come back to you!' Finally she can ask to be given 'le détail de vos plaisirs' (F389) to relieve her boredom now she is no longer 'occupée', knowing that Valmont will regard this as a meaningless automatic libertine touch long after the mask has been dropped.

The profusion of hints of her love for him assures Valmont, even more than did L.131, that the Marquise would welcome a return to the past; he has only to be true to his own forecast (L.96) and prove that to him Tourvel is the 'femme ordinaire' (F268) he wrongly anticipated she would all too quickly become, and his reward is within his grasp. A half-way house en route to the complete break with the Présidente which is being engineered—apparently at such cost to Merteuil's carefully nurtured picture of herself as the iron lady (L.81)—is the escapade with Emilie and its aftermath, but the temporary sacrifice of L.138 is insufficient to convince Merteuil of the Vicomte's good faith. Perhaps the feint of love in L.134 has worked too well, and Valmont thinks she will be satisfied with a provisional rejection of Tourvel and a show of ironic detachment. The requirement 'que [...] Mme de Tourvel ne fût plus pour vous qu'une femme ordinaire' (L.134, F387) is a somewhat vague stipulation. L.141 is more to the point: it determines what 'l'ensemble de votre conduite' (F388) entails exactly, and puts Valmont in possession of the means of sacrifice; it seems that, far from demonstrating his libertine 'énergie' (F382), he has to be passively led by the nose and shown how to dispatch his victim.

Letters 141 and 142 raise some interesting problems. What is the fatal fascination of the model dismissal letter; why is it such an inescapable challenge; how precisely does Merteuil outwit Valmont ?

L.141 holds Valmont to his word. Since it gives him the means to make the sacrifice, it is an opportunity, which he cannot sidestep, to prove that 'j'ai voulu vous réserver l'honneur de ce sacrifice' (L.138, F397) is not a self-delusion, or an attempt to pull the wool over Merteuil's eyes, behind which lurks an uncontrollable desire to keep Tourvel, the woman he loves. At the beginning of L.138, he had asserted 'non, je ne suis point amoureux; et ce n'est pas ma faute si les circonstances me forcent d'en jouer le rôle' (F396). Here is an unavoidable chance to substantiate the first part of that allegation and to expose the rest of it as unworthy of a libertine who is never the hostage to fortune, for Merteuil incorporates a version of that claim in the dismissal letter which, while effectively dictating the course of events, reads like an ironic parody of the Vicomte's words. In L.141, moreover, the Marquise accuses him of loving Tourvel with a love 'qui fait trouver à une femme les agréments ou les qualités qu'elle n'a pas' (F403). The model letter gives him the wherewithal to comply with the demand that Merteuil had imposed on him in L.134 (F387, bottom), and one particular sentence in it—'Si, par exemple, j'ai eu juste autant d'amour que toi de vertu, et c'est sûrement beaucoup dire, il n'est pas étonnant que l'un ait fini en même temps que l'autre'—affords him an opportunity to deny his love (by suggesting that the usual process of disillusionment after conquest has set in) and to fulfil his own prediction 'Ah! le temps ne viendra que trop tôt, où, dégradée par sa chute, elle ne sera plus pour moi qu'une femme ordinaire' (F268). Valmont has already committed himself to abandoning the Présidente: the inference is already there, perhaps, in L.21, F75, but the undertaking of L.115 is quite explicit: 'je la quitterai' (F335). It was by playing upon fears for his reputation (L.113, F325-6) that Merteuil extracted the promise of L.115; [24] L.141 repeats the tactic (F404) and gives him the means of proving his word. He claims he is not in love (see L.133 'Et je ne saurais pas m'en défendre!', F384) but his actions belie his words; now let him show it.

Valmont has to abandon Tourvel in a spectacular and ruthless way to show that he is the devil-may-care rake, the murderer of reputations, the man who exploits feelings and is never their prey. It is a sacrifice he can afford to make: there is no danger that Merteuil will refuse him his reward (so he thinks) since L.131 and L.134 and hints in L.141 have confirmed his long-standing prejudice that the Marquise loved him in the past and continues to love him now. Moreover, there is an enticing hint of an escape clause in the letter which Valmont uses as his model—'je te reviendrai peut-être' (F405). The desertion of Tourvel may suggest that he has exchanged one sort of emotional enslavement for another; or is there a qualitative difference between a 'passion pusillanime' (F357) for Tourvel and his supposed feelings for Merteuil (L.142) which makes the avowal of the latter not subject to the normal libertine code ? But if he can win his reward at the cost of a deceitful insinuation of his love for Merteuil (F406), then Valmont is prepared to lie, for knowing that he is only pretending to love Merteuil does not erode his libertine self-respect, whereas the (belated?) recognition that he truly loves Tourvel, with a love which outlasts the emotion of first impressions, certainly does. It is not even a clear lie, being put in the form of a rhetorical question: 'Ah! sans doute, il y en a [sc. de l'amour], et beaucoup! Mais pour qui ?' (*ibid* .) [25] The Vicomte can tell himself that with Merteuil, as with Cécile, 'je n'ai pas à me reprocher d'avoir prononcé le mot d'amour' (L.144, F410); the question in L.142 refers back to a phrase in the dismissal letter merely copied by him—'Aujourd'hui, une femme que j'aime éperdument exige que je te sacrifie' (F404). What does it signify that he lies if Merteuil is satisfied with the demonstration (the letters from her suggest she will be, for this is the test of his love which she has herself devised; cf. 'disposer de vos sentiments', F388) and if he can himself retain, perhaps, a certain private ironic detachment ?—'les plus tendres baisers de l'amour', L.142, F406, is significantly close to the formula in the old love letter ironically quoted at the end of L.125.

L.142, therefore, finds Valmont, despite having been cornered and forced into action, in a reasonably sanguine mood. He is sure of his reputation, having vindicated his self-image without compromising himself with Merteuil, sure of his reward to come as a token of her love and a final verification of his indifference to Tourvel, eagerly awaiting the latter's reaction to his bold stroke to confirm his triumph, and with the seductive phrase 'je te reviendrai peut-être' perhaps lingering at the back of his mind. Yet within a few letters he discovers that he has allowed himself to be tricked into making a sacrifice for which Merteuil very probably has no intention of repaying him, and moreover that he has himself provided her with ammunition to use against him. Merteuil's scheme to outflank him by playing up to his misconception concerning her feelings for him has become her chief preoccupation, particularly after L.125; and L.141, which plunges him into a paradoxical situation where his actions are as unproductive of the results he desires as his words had formerly been unconvincing, is the ingenious culmination of that plan. It is she who hoodwinks him, but Valmont himself must take the blame for his blindness, for unsubtle tactics, and for adding to the contradictions which trap him and baulk his hopes.

By sheer guile, Merteuil outwits the Vicomte. The embittered tone of L.141, the perspicacious analysis that, surely, hurt feelings and jealousy produce, these are effective enough devices in themselves. [26] But this letter also continues the technique of L.134 in a small way, using indirect suggestion to shore up the illusion of her love, for Merteuil is a past master in the art of the ambiguous insinuation. A phrase to be found in the preamble to the model dismissal letter—'ou peut-être encore par quelque autre motif'—can be taken in two very different ways. The whole sentence in which it occurs is this:

> Cet homme avait une amie qui fut tentée un moment de le livrer au Public en cet état d'ivresse, et de rendre ainsi son ridicule ineffaçable: mais pourtant, plus généreuse que maligne, ou peut-être encore par quelque autre motif, elle voulut tenter un dernier moyen, pour être, à tout événement, dans le cas de dire, comme son ami: *Ce n'est pas ma faute* . (F404)

No doubt Valmont is meant to understand 'ou peut-être encore' as cumulative ("or again perhaps because she was in love with him"), whereas Merteuil herself obviously regards it as adversative ("or perhaps rather because she wanted vengeance upon him by making him sacrifice this woman, without herself intending to sacrifice her chosen lover to him"). As well as hinting that her own motivation in sending him this model letter is her love for him, while secretly revelling in the mental reservation that it is quite the opposite, Merteuil allows him the choice of two motives for breaking with Tourvel which he is no doubt too impercipient to notice are so opposed as to be mutually exclusive.

The first of these is the motive of restoring his libertine image and demonstrating his freedom and lack of any emotional ties to the Présidente: this is alluded to in the part of the *mise en abyme* anecdote which reads 'il n'avait pas le courage de rompre. Son embarras était d'autant plus grand, qu'il s'était vanté à ses amis d'être entièrement libre' (F404). The second motive is that of proving his love for the Marquise: it surfaces in the letter-within-a-letter in the form 'Aujourd'hui, une femme que j'aime éperdument exige que je te sacrifie' (*ibid*.).

But the abandonment of Tourvel is ineffective immediately it is made. In Merteuil's eyes, if Valmont broke with the Présidente through a vain concern with reputation and with his own view of himself, he cannot have surrendered the woman out of any self-sacrificing love for his former partner (not that Merteuil has the emotional involvement with him to be impressed if he had done so): love and self-love seem necessarily to exclude each other. The speed with which he responds to the devastating analysis of F403 and to the challenge of 'il n'avait pas le courage de rompre' suggests not that Valmont, as a tactic to win his reward, has forced Merteuil, by a pretence of love for Tourvel, into demanding a sacrifice which he is quite unconcerned about making, but that it can only be love for the Présidente which is such a grave threat to his libertine self-respect that he has to sacrifice her so peremptorily, [27] thereby plunging himself into the contradiction that he proves he is a free agent by enslaving himself to Merteuil's will.

Moreover, the Vicomte adds to the contradictions with which he is surrounded by proposing a possible reconciliation with Tourvel in L.144. In fact the ideas of 'amour [...] pour qui ?'(L.142) and 'raccommodement' (F409) cancel each other out. He cannot be in love with Merteuil, even though he has sacrificed Tourvel for her, if he wants to go back to 'la belle délaissée' (F408), no matter how carefully he presents the idea of a reconciliation: therefore he must have sacrificed the Présidente to his vanity and now deeply regrets doing so. ("Why should a woman bother herself with a man who sacrifices love to vanity ?" is a useful polemical point to keep in reserve for the future). In L.145 the Marquise has an additional reason for ignoring the 'amour [...] pour qui?' argument, apart from the obvious one that she does not love him, and that is that Valmont has sabotaged its tenuous credibility himself. She is all the more determined to refuse him his reward and to go off with Danceny, after rubbing Valmont's nose in the uncomfortable truth (F411-12).

Following L.142, the Vicomte is in an over-confident state of mind, as normal (see L.99). He is so persuaded of the effectiveness of sending the proxy letter as a ploy to win his reward, that in L.144 (F410) he talks of giving back Cécile to Danceny, not because he at last realises the true implications of his being allowed to keep the girl (L.134, F388), but because he thinks he can afford to return her to her young lover now that the Marquise is about to take her place as the provider of sexual largesse. What is more, he has no suspicions that 'je te reviendrai peut-être' (F405) may very well have been a deliberate "plant" by Merteuil to make the sending of the dismissal letter a more attractive proposition to him. To the Vicomte there is no contradiction between L.142 and L.144 if he can present his idea of a reconciliation with the Présidente as if it were purely another libertine project which is eminently worthy of a libertine's approval. He dresses it up as 'un simple essai que nous ferions de concert' (F409): to manipulate in different directions an emotional weakling whom he has crushed and who is like putty in his hands (notice the dismissive use of 'on', *ibid.*). This is a scheme of benefit to the Marquise since it can produce a further tribute, for there is no reason why Tourvel should not be cast off a second time and her feelings once more trampled underfoot. It is as if he regards it as an intellectual challenge to see if it is possible to make 'je te reviendrai peut-être' in the model letter come true against all the odds—despite the fact that such a 'raccommodement' has been cynically forecast in the instrument of dismissal itself. As regards the invitation to Merteuil : 'Venez donc vite retrouver votre Amant, vos plaisirs, vos amis, et le courant des aventures' (F409), Valmont, who in reality is deluded by the Marquise's feint of love and jealousy and by her apparently hankering after a monogamous relationship, thinks that if he *pretends* to believe that Merteuil will not of course be returning to Paris to devote herself single-mindedly to one lover (himself), so, conversely, she will be in no position to object to his non-exclusive interest in her, and will give him leeway to pursue the Présidente once more. Not, of course, that he is exclusively devoted to the lady; far from it, for is he not also interested in a little 'expérience' with Cécile ? The twinning of the two projects, the juxtaposition of the 'essai' and the 'expérience' is intended to suggest that Valmont's feelings are not engaged with Tourvel—how can they be, for he has proved his love for Merteuil in L.142 ?—though he is treading on dangerous ground, for this vocabulary recalls 'observation' in L.133.

The precise mistake Valmont commits in L.144 could, no doubt, be defined in a number of different ways: is it to include in the letter, naively and quite unconsciously, an indication of his abiding fascination with the Présidente which undermines the point of his sacrifice ? Or to use contradictory tactics in trying to get Merteuil to return to give him his reward? These are cajolement, then pressure—first proving his love for the Marquise by dismissing Tourvel, then throwing doubt on the proof so that Merteuil will supposedly come hurrying back to Paris 'pour [le] fixer', to stop him joining forces with Tourvel again. Or is his miscalculation to think that he can dress up the project to renew with the Présidente with a libertine presentation and in such a way as to make it difficult for Merteuil to object ? Taken together, Letters 142 and 144, in our estimation, show the Vicomte's rather desultory attempt to ride, to his own advantage, the twin horses of Merteuil's love and her libertine image. But Merteuil is driven by a single, singular, and ungovernable animal—the desire for vengeance and the will to dominate—and Valmont is already destined to come a cropper. L.145 marks the beginning of the end. Merteuil, who has humiliated Valmont with an antiphrastic 'surrender' 'à [son] vainqueur' (F411) when she has cornered him into making a pointless unilateral sacrifice, now has every reason to pursue Danceny and deny Valmont his reward, and nothing the Vicomte can do can persuade her to abandon her advantage; so that when he finds her with her young "pupil" (L.151, F426) the tables are turned, another lover is now preferred to him just as he had preferred Tourvel to her, and without reciprocal sacrifices the final clash is inevitable.

Setting aside the savage irony and the triumphalist tone, L.145's analysis is essentially correct: Valmont has sacrificed his love for Mme de Tourvel to his vanity; and his later efforts to counteract the effects of the dismissal letter bear witness to a despairing realisation that he has lost his love and the best part of himself out of a concern for appearances and a trumpery vainglory. They are not, it can be fairly assumed, a sign that he is merely rising to a libertine challenge to prove the Marquise wrong in her prognosis 'Ah! croyez-moi, Vicomte, quand une femme frappe dans le cœur d'une autre, elle manque rarement de trouver l'endroit sensible, et la blessure est incurable' (L.145, F412).

*****

Is Merteuil wrong in L.145 to insist that Valmont has sacrificed his love for the Présidente to his vanity ? Did Laclos cut the original version of L.155 (F493) because he saw it was possible to maintain that Valmont had never loved Tourvel and never really regretted abandoning her ? Some readers may feel that Valmont, in his bid to hurt the Marquise, whom he takes to be jealous, and to play upon her feelings, even after L.125 is merely *impersonating* the role of Mme de Tourvel's lover. Does he drop hints of his love for the Présidente (through unreliable denials, temporary sacrifices, etc.) so that he can manipulate Merteuil into explicitly demanding an apparently impossible sacrifice which he has absolutely no compunction about making; does he skilfully project the illusion of his love for Tourvel at the Marquise so as to induce her to make a request which he can quite painlessly fulfil and thereby win his reward? Surely the swiftness with which Valmont reacts to the challenge of L.141 to substantiate his assertion that he is only acting the part of the lover of Tourvel (L.138) shows how unconvincing he senses the claim to be, and how important it is to quell the notion (and therefore how likely it is) that he is identifying too closely with his role. If the whole point of pretending to love the Présidente is to barter her for his reward after forcing a sacrifice, why does he ruin all his best efforts by continuing to "pretend" to be so much in love with Tourvel that he wishes for a reconciliation with her (L.144), so that Merteuil has an excuse to discount his sacrifice and go off with Danceny ? Despite the presentation of F409, and indeed because of the conspicuous care taken to distract attention from the fact that his feelings rather than his intellect require the reconciliation, it is perfectly plain that Valmont has a fatal obsession with the Présidente which outlasts his sacrifice.

The real infatuation perhaps begins in L.100.[28] There is an authentic note of 'odi et amo' about this letter, and what the Vicomte feels is not just the illusion of love produced by thwarted desire. Laclos originally wrote 'quelle fatalité m'a fait désirer cette femme' (variant 'e', V1314, top), but the much stronger correction 'quelle fatalité m'attache à cette femme?' (F286) leads the reader away from the idea that what is involved is merely frustrated desire. The answer to the question 'Pourquoi courir après celui [sc. le plaisir] qui nous fuit, et négliger ceux qui se présentent ? Ah ! pourquoi ?...' (F287) lies not in the 'obstacle mechanism' of the libertine noted by Henri Duranton, [29] but in the special attractions of Tourvel to a 'cœur flétri' (F46). While Valmont's feelings in L.100 are a subtle blend of passionate obsession and libertine rage at the baulking of his desire to dominate and impose his will, it is evident that he is breaking the code of the libertine in disregarding 'l'attrait de la variété, le charme des nouvelles conquêtes, l'éclat de leur nombre' (F287), singling out one woman as worth all the rest, and preferring quality to quantity; [30] moreover, in his wish to see the Présidente 'livrée aux orages que j'éprouve en ce moment' (*ibid*.), all the associations connected with our mental picture of Mme de Tourvel seem to determine that 'orages' refers more to the emotions of love than to the rage of will-power deflected from its path.

Once Valmont has won the Présidente he finds it increasingly difficult to confer any credibility on the line of defence that his dealings with her show him to be a true libertine playing upon the emotions of his victim while remaining detached and unsullied by passion himself; at the same time the theory that he may be manipulating a supposedly loving ex-partner by a *calculated* semblance of weakness and a pretence of love for his latest conquest is, as we have suggested, not easy to follow through. In order to prove he is not attached to Tourvel, he has to force himself to go off and make love to Emilie and to write the dismissal letter knowing it is lies, but the reconciliation of L.138 and the projected reunion with her after the sacrifice (L.144) simply prove he is. "Having" the Présidente has not saved him from the 'ridicule d'en être amoureux' (L.4, F41). 'Volupté' never manages to 'détacher le bandeau de l'amour' (L.6, F44). His feeling for her is not just frustrated desire, for when desire achieves its object, and satiety sets in, it turns to disgust, and beauty and all attractions fade and are finally recognised as a subjective delusion (L.131 demonstrates that mere sexual desire can never be the basis for a lasting relationship).

No—his feeling for her is love which endows her person and his contact with her with a 'charme inconnu' and makes her anything but a 'femme ordinaire'. He has artificially to coerce himself into copying out the model letter which includes the lying excuse that his love ended when she stopped virtuously resisting him; artificially to dragoon himself into dismissing her therefore as a 'femme ordinaire' who is 'dégradée par sa chute' all too soon (F286), for the fact is that his prediction of L.96 has *not* proved correct, the 'charme inconnu' is never convincingly denied, and love would have sustained the relationship far longer than a month, had vanity allowed. The affair itself is a long time reaching fulfilment. In the course of a protracted courtship we can say variously that Valmont is only prolonging the chase, thinking that he can put off the usual disappointment that ensues when desire reaches its goal, luxuriating in a 'sentiment inconnu' which postpones the necessity for sexual possession, or finding arguments—in the conception of a delayed, consciously-controlled campaign against virtue—to rationalise a lover's timidity. But in truth, when finally he does possess Tourvel the expected disillusionment does not materialise, and Valmont is obliged, for his libertine peace of mind, to pretend that it has.

Laclos suppressed the original L.155 which, seen in isolation in the appendix (F493-4), is as clear a statement of Valmont's love for Mme de Tourvel and of his regret at what he has done to her as one could hope to have (v. 'en l'assurant de mon repentir, de mes regrets, et surtout de mon amour', F493). The critics tell us that Laclos removed L.155 (O.S.) precisely because it was too clear-cut a declaration of the Vicomte's feelings and too final a rejection of his libertinism. Versini believes that Laclos 'a préféré [...] éviter à Valmont de se déclarer de façon édifiante pour le bien' (V1392, n. 2, ref. to p. 352 of his text); Pomeau, referring to the same crossed out MS letter says 'En s'humiliant ainsi, Valmont paraissait s'engager sans retour du côté de son amour. Laclos a préféré maintenir l'équivoque'. [31] However, if we replace the letter in the narrative, it takes on a very different meaning from the one which it has when relegated to the back of the book. Following on the heels of Merteuil's declaration of war and written the very same day as it (see V1391, variant 'd', ref. to V352) Valmont's original letter could very easily be interpreted as insincere, and as nothing more than a crude attempt to use any means available to win back Tourvel simply in order to prove Merteuil wrong in her prediction that 'la blessure est incurable' (L.145, F412)—the context and the dating suggest that for Valmont the Présidente is merely a pawn in the deadly chess game with his arch rival Merteuil which is now in its final throes. Is it not possible that the original L.155 was excluded from the printed text precisely because in context it threw doubt on the sincerity of Valmont's feelings for the Présidente, seemed to justify Mme de Volanges's suspicions of his sincerity (or rather became ambiguous because the reader has been forewarned by Volanges's doubts not to take it at face value), and thus appeared to give credibiity to a cynical and one-sided interpretation of the end of the new L.155 ? [32]

How does the reader respond to the text in the form it has come down to us, when his instincts and the drift of the book tell him there can be no doubt about Valmont's feelings ? Leaving the sincerity of Valmont's despair in doubt on the hearsay of Mme de Volanges has the effect of making the reader dismiss these doubts as those of an utterly unperceptive observer (cf. L.98, L.175) who, as usual, cannot see what is under her very nose, namely that Valmont is obviously taking desperate steps to try to recover the woman whom he recognises as the love of his life. Nor may the reader feel particularly kindly disposed towards the "rédacteur",[33] who, apart from alienating him elsewhere with his moralising, has deprived him of the evidence on which to assess the validity of Mme de Volanges's doubts. He may well feel tempted to have recourse to more reliable authorities for an opinion on whether the rest of the correspondence (L.155, F436-7, is evidently being singled out by the footnote to L.154) can resolve Volanges's uncertainty. It is gratifying to find Philip Thody and Jean-Luc Seylaz unhesitating on this point:

> there is no reason to doubt the sincerity of the remark 'croyez-moi, on n'est heureux que par l'amour', with which [Valmont] ends his letter to Danceny (155). He does not need to introduce this idea in order to convince Danceny of the advantages to be derived from temporarily abandoning Madame de Merteuil for Cécile...[34]

N'oublions pas enfin le:

> Ah! croyez-moi, on n'est heureux que par l'amour (155).

> Dans le contexte, on peut y lire, sous la plume de Valmont, un aveu calculé mais sincère. [35]

*****

Any interpretation of the Valmont-Merteuil relationship which can claim to be something more than a second-hand compendium of critical commonplaces whose substantiation in the text has long been forgotten will commit itself to views on the following: Mme de Merteuil's motivation in writing L.20, and Valmont's idea of her purpose in striking the bargain it contains; Valmont's reception of L.81 and L.113; his posture and line of approach in the series of letters from L.125 to L.144; the complexities of L.133; and, finally, the appropriateness of Merteuil's remarks in L.145.

It has been my purpose in this chapter not to attempt to sidestep what must be regarded as the central cruces of the novel, but rather to confront these problems head-on, and deal with them through the application of a single and, I hope, consistent reading.

Feminism and Film

The unfair advantage which men have in the war of the sexes (see L.81), the fate of the three young women in Prévan's triple affair (see L.79), the inconsistencies in society noted by Mme de Volanges in L.32, the distinction in the case of men between inconstancy and infidelity which does not apply to women (L.130), and society's toleration of a double standard—a different sexual morality and conception of honour for men and women, however cushioned by hypocritical expedients—all these things are simply aspects of the way the cards are heavily stacked against women in the eighteenth-century world. Mme de Merteuil is in revolt against such an inequitable situation.

It is possible to argue—as Anne-Marie Jaton convincingly does—that male libertines attempt to lower and "debauch" women in the name of moral values which they implicitly recognise at the same time as they mock them: [1] to increase their reputation as seducers of women they need to obtain society's open moral condemnation of their victims.[2] True libertines need to attract responsible women who acknowledge their freedom but confess their attraction and voluntarily become slaves. In the process of seducing them they trample moral values underfoot, but then finally reject these women as "tainted" and endorse the moral denunciation by society of their victims. [3] Male libertinism, whereby the man determines to be the master and the woman must be a voluntary slave, reflects the social structures of a society where women were dependent on men. Mme de Merteuil's female libertinism reverses the roles, and under the cover of passive feminity she takes the initiative and subjugates her own victims (upsetting an ingrained idea of the natural law of the supremacy of the strong over the weak). [4]

The Prévan affair is an example of what Merteuil is attempting to do in her private revolt, and it is a nothing less than a total reversal of the sexual norm in affairs. Women are timid, docile, *sensible* —very well, she will pretend to be so. She acts towards Prévan as he had decided to act towards her. [5] He thinks he is "having" her, whereas in reality he is the real prey and she "has" him (and "has him on"). He thinks he is attacking—in fact it is she who is doing the attacking. She scores because she knows that the art of the male seducer is acquired by practice and becomes a purely mechanistic pattern of pursuit; she presents all the right symptoms and deceives him into thinking that he is getting close to the prey, but she is simply luring him on. She upsets the usual table of values and reverses the terms: what is conventionally "defeat" for the woman becomes her "victory".[6]

Society tolerates male libertinage, it is said, because male libertines exercise power and authority in a parallel way to society. Mme de Merteuil's female libertinism is an attack on male domination, whether sexual or social, and indirectly it is a revolt against the principle of authority. Through her actions and through L.81, Merteuil attacks male hegemony in a society which reduces women to protected and cosseted enslavement, or to solitary rebellion (as in her own case). [7] The Prévan incident shows that the power which libertines think the physical possession of women gives them is illusory—for Merteuil "has" Prévan and not the other way round—illusory, and a reflection of the arbitrary power which society gives men over women through laws and double-standard morality. [8]

Merteuil lucidly seeks pleasure in ephemeral relationships and rejects love as a trap in which men tyrannise women and turn them into emotional slaves; she thus protects herself against all humiliation and suffering and preserves her freedom.

L.152 is the climax of Merteuil's personal revolt; forced to choose between Danceny and Valmont, she refuses to submit to Valmont (whom, it is argued, she really loves) because she would be losing her freedom, turning into a slave, almost a married slave. She would have to submit to Valmont knowing he really loved another; she would thanklessly have to play the role of the deserted wife, for Valmont would inevitably treat her as he had treated Mme de Tourvel whom he sacrificed to his vanity.

Yet where does the Marquise's private revolt get her ? Is she more justified in what she does than that heroine of female subservience, Mme de Tourvel ? Not if she herself fails too—not if the choice of her freedom over her love (if that is what it is) [9] for Valmont leads to a fatal struggle in which both rival libertines' plans for supremacy are checkmated (conversely the Présidente's preference for love over freedom has fatal results). Nothing Merteuil does can detract from the fact that certain women (like Tourvel) perversely find a greater happiness in giving themselves to men knowing that this is the very thing which compromises their freedom and happiness.[10] Mme de Merteuil claims she is 'née pour venger mon sexe et maîtriser le vôtre' (L.81), but she cannot fulfil that goal if the form her revolt takes is the adoption of a *male* role, for how can she avenge her sex if she becomes a pseudo-man herself ? [11] In her affairs she appears to be perpetuating the hegemony of masculine values, and her rejection of passive feminity entails the domination and humiliation or exposure of *female* as well as male victims, because Cécile and the Vicomtesse de M*** (see L.74) are without doubt victims of her vanity, and she shows little solidarity with her own sex. Besides, how can she 'venger [mon] sexe et maîtriser le [vôtre]' (F221) if she has to keep her 'réputation. [...] pure'? (*ibid* .) In other words, if she accepts the double standard, in no way can her triumphs be publicly acknowledged; her vanity mirror is unfortunately a man, and obviously private recognition of her triumphs from Valmont is going to be grudging (see the beginning of L.96), filtered through a basic masculine scepticism about women, and at the mercy of Valmont's wounded pride. To be really revolutionary, Merteuil needs to create a whole subversive clan of female libertines with a masculine sense of honour like herself, but she gives up the single attempt to make Cécile her understudy and some readers may think that it is not so much because Cécile is poor material for a 'femme révoltée' as out of jealousy that Cécile is Valmont's property and in love with the man on whom she has set eyes—Danceny.

It is indeed somewhat paradoxical, not to say inconsistent, that Merteuil should end up protesting in the name of the victims of egotistical, insensitive, vain male libertines (see the end of L.152) when she had aped male libertine values in her own sexual affairs throughout the book [12] (though no doubt any argument to hand is good enough when it comes to refusing Valmont his reward). [13] Moreover, the failure of her personal revolt owing to male complicity (Valmont and Danceny's arrangements after the duel which lead to her social exposure) simply re-endorses the hypocritical values of a male-dominated society: [14] Prévan is rehabilitated and applauded as a replacement for Valmont, while Merteuil is ostracised by society women slavishly subscribing to the view that women must at all costs preserve the *appearance* of virtue. Readers will remember that Prévan and Merteuil had both wanted the same thing, and some may feel that in absolute moral terms if one was dishonourable and dishonoured then so was the other. The "typically masculine", war-orientated, "conquer or perish" [15] psychology of relationships viewed as an inevitable power struggle, following which Merteuil fights her last battle with Valmont, is finally exposed as barren, for neither the Vicomte nor the Marquise wins; both depart from the scene, leaving the reader with the memory of the magnificent but futile altruism of Tourvel, and—equally vain—the heroic struggle of Merteuil to control her own destiny. This is a woman who is really beaten from the start by the system; if her essentially private revolt needs a witness, Valmont moves beyond being her recalcitrant vanity mirror to becoming posthumously a witness to the hypocritical world of her perhaps understandable, but ultimately ineffectual, maliciousness.

In all of this Laclos may be criticising a society which, for as long as it continues to deny freedom to the average woman, only offers her exceptional sister two choices—the heroic assumption of her slavery, or the self-indulgence of a purely private revolt that is, by the nature of things, limited in scope, however effectively it parodies the objectivisations of male desire. A more "typically feminist" reading of his novel, however, would no doubt claim that (male) seduction had never been made more enticing, and that never had women been presented in a less flattering light than in *Les Liaisons dangereuses* . [16]

*****

Stephen Frear's award-winning film *Dangerous Liaisons* opened to considerable critical acclaim and has recently (March 1989) gone on general release in Great Britain. Alan Frank is typical of the popular critics in finding it:

> ... a film which catalyses the intellect while at the same time ravishing the eye. The sexual melodrama it sets up and solves very satisfactorily may be artificial but, within the confines of the film, it makes for two hours of beautifully acted adult entertainment. [17]

Face-to-face encounters between characters by and large take the place in the film of letter-writing in the novel, or of telephone conversations in Vadim's earlier, modern-dress filmed version (*Les Liaisons dangereuses* , 1960). Letters are used in the title sequence and a bundle of letters tied up in lace, which Valmont apparently carries on his person even when duelling, is sufficient to have Merteuil booed at the Comédie Italienne at the end. Which ones ? we wonder, since the damning L.81 has already been converted into an on-screen tête-à-tête. But apart from the place which the delivery of letters retains in the dual seduction, apart from L.48 and an ingenious variation on the same idea (Cécile in bed with Valmont, writing L.117 to Danceny under dictation from the Vicomte and employing his naked back as a desk), the appearance of letters is, out of visual necessity, somewhat underplayed in the film. The dramatisation of the act of letter-writing is always kept for special effects. It makes a visually interesting scene to have Cécile faint in a heap when her mother, alerted by Merteuil, discovers the letters she has been exchanging with Danceny—no need to waste time on any details of the insipid correspondence itself. Moreover, no attempt is made to translate the multiple viewpoint of the letter novel into visual terms; it is probably just as well, since the average film-goer will surely find that, as it is, a continual effort of concentration is needed if one is to be able to follow the details of the plot, without having to suffer the added complication of a fragmented view.

In the title sequence Frear's film seems to be presented as an adaptation of an adaptation, since it is described there as 'based on the play adapted from the novel'. Devotees of Laclos's book might therefore be expected to complain that, as such, it can be no more faithful to the original than is Jean-Jacques Annaud's *The Name of the Rose* , which justifies the liberties it takes by styling itself, rather archly, 'a palimpsest of the novel'. Fortunately for us, Christopher Hampton, who was responsible for the play still running so successfully at the Ambassadors Theatre, London, as well as for the screenplay of the film, is a genuine Laclos enthusiast. In the event, his screenplay is remarkably skilful in adapting the book and turning it into a piece of popular entertainment—particularly in its recasting of the first twenty and final fifty letters—while preserving much of the spirit of the original.

Changes are ruthlessly made for the sake of simplifying the plot and concentrating on the main characters and their interaction. The anecdotes are removed or modified. Prévan, his sexual athleticism, his encounter with Merteuil and his reappearance at the end, do not feature at all in the film, and the ironic view of society's hypocrisy in the different treatment it accords to Prévan and Merteuil is sacrificed. Neatly, Mme de Volanges takes over the role of the Vicomtesse de M***, appointing Valmont as lover for the night in preference to Vressac or her husband (compare L.71). This incident, which Valmont recounts to Cécile so that she will lose respect for her mother, is now set some fifteen or sixteen years in the past, before the birth of Cécile. Added piquancy is given to Valmont's seduction of the girl by the faint hint of incest, while her miscarriage seems partly her own fault—a punishment for her naivety—since she has been forewarned of 'a few elementary precautions to be taken' by Merteuil, who appears in person to advise her. In the book, Valmont deliberately keeps the girl in the dark. He brings Merteuil written proof of Tourvel's surrender ('she writes as badly as she dresses'), where no such letter exists in the novel; this helps to explain his anger when Merteuil fails to keep her part of the bargain. Instead of dismissing Tourvel from a distance by sending her a second-hand letter, the Vicomte confronts her face to face in a scene where he pulls no punches, and which, dramatically speaking, pulls no punches either, since it powerfully spotlights his subservience to Merteuil, the struggle between vanity and love within him, and the ensuing sadistic cruelty of which only he is capable. Perhaps on the supposition that these omissions neutralise the notion of an arbitrary Providence, suddenly at work in what is essentially a drama of human weakness, there is in the film no court case to be lost, nor smallpox to afflict Merteuil after her social disgrace.

One or two changes or additions seem unnecessary, however. Gercourt becomes 'Bastide'—perhaps because it was thought that this was a more distinctive and memorable name for a character who never appears in the film. Some fairly crude examples of *double entendre* crop up: Cécile will soon be 'back in the saddle'; Azolan is urged to 'keep it up'; Emilie has 'nothing firm for tonight'.

The château setting and the suitably aged, apparently stone-washed costumes are lovingly photographed; every rustle made by yards of material being transported and compressed into the furniture is faithfully recorded at normal level on the sound-track. Glenn Close appears as an appropriately mature, commanding Merteuil, alternately gracious and steely; her long-jawed, square, determined features are nevertheless sufficiently malleable in close-up to convey gradations of feeling, as when Valmont relates the joys of his success with Tourvel and the impression it left on him. The film audience is never allowed to doubt that the Marquise is in love with Valmont, and accepts that her libertinism and rivalry, while appearing as a convenient mask to protect her feelings, are ultimately not reconcilable with them. Coming after the duel and before the final shock of her discovery that society is ostracising her, there is an invented scene, not based on anything in the novel, in which Merteuil, sweeping things off her dressing table, rages with dramatic anguish and despair at Valmont's death.

The strength of the film, in fact, lies in its straightforward portrayal of strong characters and their emotions, and in its simplification of psychological ambiguities. We can forgive John Malkovich his rather camp manner, mesmeric undertone, the touches of Jack Nicholson at his most demonic, and the moments of unintentionally self-conscious acting (as if aware of himself in fancy dress under the eye of a camera, not of eighteenth-century society), for overall he gives a performance of real power and manages to suggest the animal-like menace of Valmont by his way of stalking his victim, then pouncing on her like a bird of prey. There is no doubt that the character falls in love with his victim and is made fully to pay for his desertion of her. The first hint of any real recognition of his love can perhaps be found in his self-accusation of insensitivity, after staging the confrontation of Emilie and Tourvel; here he pretends to be merely funding Emilie's "charitable work", a very different version in the film from L.138 in the text. At the end, the duel is intercut with shots of Tourvel pining away, near to death, in her bed in the convent, juxtaposed with Valmont's fond memories of the two lovers in bed together. In a moment of apparent mental absence, remembering his happiness with her, he drops his sword and is cut down by Danceny, who is then made the intermediary to convey Valmont's undying love and repudiation of his dismissal of Tourvel to the dying woman herself: this version may be compared and contrasted with letters 154, 163 and 165. Hence the film puts the final emphasis on the sentimental element and on the fact that it takes precedence over the intellectual, whereas literary critics can argue that the novel leaves open the possibility that Merteuil's feelings for Valmont, and even Valmont's for Tourvel, are never entirely authentic or credible.

Conclusion

Les Liaisons dangereuses could be described as the story of revenge (as we suggested in our introductory chapter), or of love's revenge. All the characters who have the time and the opportunity to fall in love are forbidden to love by their situation or by the self-imposed codes by which ideally they would live their lives—that is according to "principles" understood in the conventional sense of the word, or in a very different one. Danceny is supposed to be a celibate knight of Malta; [1] Cécile and Tourvel must avert their eyes from any other partner but their legitimate husband or husband-to-be; to Valmont and the Marquise de Merteuil, love is a sentimental delusion, an unforgivable weakness, a source of derision. Yet all but Merteuil fall victim to what either system views as the weakness of love, and this is the beginning of their fall from grace in the sense that, having once succumbed in spirit, they are ready to be manipulated emotionally or through their vanity to reap love's more tangible rewards (with disastrous consequences), or open to attack from the side of their self-respect by whoever mocks their feelings. Even Merteuil herself has to pay the price for valuing a form of love—self-love—above all else. Moreover the Vicomte and the Marquise could with a certain justice be regarded as victims of their inability to love with any capacity for constancy or self-sacrifice (v. *supra* , the chapter on Moral). Love, then, wreaks a terrible vengeance, alike on those who indulge it, disregard it, or betray it.

Laclos's novel is also an exercise in ironic mimicry. Merteuil taunts Valmont and leads him into a trap by mimicking a sentimental nostalgia about her past relationship with him, yet ultimately is forced to pay, by a social disgrace which cannot be laughed off, for her refusal to resurrect an affair which she was only feigning to look back on with longing. With a judicious smattering of parodic *bienséant* attitudes at times (L.32; L.104) she mimics a Providence, which, through the infusion of grace—or, in her case, of commonplace notions of righteousness—directs individual wills to serve its ends; yet, in a way both providential and very unprovidential, at the end of the day is brought down by the contingency of events. Valmont apes the language of sentiment (bluffing the Présidente, for example, with a piece of passionate tropology which is all too unfigurative [L.48]), yet ends up trapped in his role-playing, and unable to disassociate his real feelings from the part he is playing. As regards the book's structure, one affair mimics another, and the parallel patterns of relationship suggest, sometimes ironically, the irresistibility of passion at all levels, or contrast power with the illusion of power.

As the dénouement makes plain, *Les Liaisons dangereuses* is concerned with characters ruled by the imperious demands of their self-image, characters who fail to live up to their self-image, or who are overruled by this failure. Cécile retreats to a convent for fear of the exposure of the falsity of her image as a conventional, well-bred convent girl. Embarrassed by Valmont's leering references to his new career 'courant les aventures' (L.155 and L.157), out of sensitivity over his self-image as an honest sentimental lover, the antithesis of the Don Juan type, Danceny is manoeuvred into going back to Cécile and deserting Merteuil for the night, thus fatally embroiling himself in the mutual revenge of the Marquise and the Vicomte. Mme de Volanges is moved, out of *bien-pensant* self-respect, to refuse to help Valmont restore the Présidente to life (L.154), and ends the book helplessly wringing her hands and purveying laughably blind platitudes. Mme de Rosemonde, manipulated by her self-image as the only defender of a worthy aristocratic line and the repository of family honour, is led to indulge in some spectacular hypocrisies with Danceny (L.171), and to keep the family skeleton securely in the cupboard by not releasing during her lifetime documents she has gathered which might incriminate her nephew. Mme de Tourvel repudiates her self-image as a virtuous married woman, enters another world of passionate values, and entirely loses her self-respect when Valmont fails to respond to her sacrifice with undying fidelity, scorns her devotion, and condemns her, as she had foreseen, in the name of the moral values she had abandoned for him.[2] Priding himself on his skill in intellectual penetration as a preliminary to sexual success, the Vicomte totally misreads Merteuil's mind, and, by L.145, finds himself hopelessly outmanoeuvred. Merteuil's self-image as the domineering master of men, playthings whom she can break with impunity (L.81), induces her to overplay her hand and try to crush Valmont when the letters she has sent him have not been secured, while Valmont's image as the uncaring rake despising feelings has provoked him to abandon the only love of his life. Self-image is the internalisation of a prevailing social value—*paraître*—and when appearance and reality can no longer be distinguished on the private stage, short-sighted self-deception is usually waiting in the wings to trap the unwary, for it is the inevitable concomitant of spiritual pride.

This is a collection of letters characterised by variety—of viewpoints and shifting perspectives, of characters and of styles reflecting character; it is a tapestry of motifs and recurring ideas and their variations ('confiance', 'principes', 'expériences / observation', 'ce n'est pas ma faute', and the like), a correspondence woven at times out of self-reference and purely verbal links [3]—a contexture coloured by frequently ironic medical, religious, legal, educational, theatrical and military imagery—and always self-justifying in every sense of the term. Yet in the midst of variety, one underlying theme returns like a leitmotiv: these characters have a propensity for vanity which cannot be denied. Indeed so susceptible are they that vanity is the real Achilles heel of all of them—even the apparently invulnerable. Cécile loses her virginity to Valmont, but she is not corrupted and thoroughly "debauched" by him, until, that is, she takes the proffered lure that she might eventually use him to launch herself in fashionable society (F305). Danceny is no doubt unconsciously seduced by the thought of his attractiveness to Merteuil even if circumstances conspire to separate him from Cécile. Tourvel is brought down by a form of spiritual pride: in the vain hope of having the glory of converting a notorious sinner conferred on her name, she overestimates her powers of virtuous resistance. Valmont and the Marquise eliminate each other because out of an exaggerated sense of injury to their self-respect and image they cannot call a truce and stop short of turning their rivalry into a fight to the finish.

Let us concentrate our attention, finally, on the latter pair, the chief protagonists of the book. Paradoxically, sexual realism and the freedom of libertinage and sexual liberation imply enslavement to yet another idol (self-image), the determinism of having to refuse emotional commitment at all costs, and the final manipulation of the unacceptability of being oneself manipulated. Unable to transcend their sexist view of relationships between men and women as master-slave affairs, these are heroes who determine, through the deification of intelligence, to dominate destiny and control their victims by pulling the strings of emotion—in a word, to become the fate of others. But manipulated by their self-image with its no less irrational demands, and trapped by their roles as supreme puppet-masters, they become themselves the puppets of fate, themselves 'le jouet de [leurs] caprices' (F221). Whether or not we are prepared to generalise from such a false

140

sense of their fitness to control events and bend others to their will as far as to see it as the common failing of their class, we cannot deny the grandeur of Laclos's portrayal of hubris thwarted ultimately by human weakness and miscalculation. Love, vanity, chance or fate: it is this fatal trio which presides over the plot of a work by genre of its time, and in scope of universal tragic resonance. What more fitting metaphor can there be for chance infiltrating, undercutting, subverting the conscious calculations of intelligence, than that Laclos family tradition according to which *Les Liaisons dangereuses* was written on a *tric-trac* board which Pierre-Ambroise-François took with him on military service ?

Notes on 'Problems and Preliminaries'

(1)   Laclos, *Œuvres complètes* , ed. Laurent Versini, NRF Gallimard, "Bibliothèque de la Pléiade", 1979. L. Versini, *Laclos et la tradition* , Klincksieck, 1968. Please note that the place of publication is Paris or London, unless otherwise indicated. I have kept abbreviations to a minimum in the introduction, so as to avoid unnecessary complications for the reader. 'F' followed by a number, means that the page to which reference is made is in the Folio edition of *Les Liaisons dangereuses* (Préface d'André Malraux; notice et notes de Joël Papadopoulos, Gallimard, 1972); since it is more widely available, it is referred to more frequently than the irreplaceable Versini edition. 'L.' refers to the particular letter. Abbreviated references to other editions are not made until the second chapter and thereafter: see Ch. 2, note 1. Full page references are given for separate articles not listed in my Bibliography.

For the social context within which the book was written and for the type of the libertine, see the useful summary in Jean-Luc Faivre, *Les Liaisons dangereuses: Laclos* , Hatier, 'Profil d'une œuvre', 1973, pp. 13-16. There is a chicken-and-egg argument about whether the literary type of the *roué* reflects the actual social type or vice versa, but see Versini ed., p. 1189, n. 2 to p. 26 of Versini's text. For Versac, v. Lloyd Free, 'Crébillon fils, Laclos, and the code of the libertine', in *Eighteenth-Century Life* , I (1974), 36-40.

(2)   Mainly through sheer repetition. Consult the following: Jean Rousset, *Forme et signification* , José Corti, 1967, pp. 65-108; *id.*, 'Les lecteurs indiscrets', in *Laclos et le libertinage* , PUF, "Publications du centre d'études du roman et du romanesque; Université de Picardie", 1983, pp. 89-96; L. Versini, *Le Roman épistolaire* , PUF, "Littératures modernes", 1979, ch. 8; René Pomeau, *Laclos* , Hatier, 1975, ch. 6, pp. 70-86; Faivre, pp. 51-4; Simon Davies, *Laclos: 'Les Liaisons dangereuses'* , Grant & Cutler Ltd., "Critical guides to French texts ", 68, 1987, pp. 42-50; Henri Blanc, *'Les liaisons dangereuses' de Choderlos de Laclos* , Hachette, "Poche critique", 1972, pp. 23-6; 36-51; Yvon Belaval, *Choderlos de Laclos* , Seghers, 1972, pp. 41-2. See also B. Duyfhuizen, 'Epistolary narratives of transmission and transgression', in *Comparative Literature* , 37, 1 (1985), 1-25.

(3)   *Choderlos de Laclos ou l'obstination* , Grasset, 1985.

(4)   The Folio edition is not without blemish. The following is a short list of the more important corrections that need to be made to the text:

F326 'je ne vois pas que votre retour y puisse nuire'; F402 'par un libertinage d'esprit'; F409 'Il y aura donc entre nous deux'; F464 'on gémit souvent'; F467 'je conçois qu'il serait possible que ma surveillance eût été trompée, et je redoute que ma fille, séduite, n'ait mis le comble à ses égarements'; F471 'l'orgueil de vouloir que vous ne pussiez en douter. J'espère que vous pardonnerez cette délicatesse'.

The translation of P.W.K. Stone (Penguin Classics, 1981) is in general excellent. Inadvertently, however, a number of (mainly printing) errors have crept in. These are listed here for the benefit of those students studying the novel in this, the most widely used English version:

L.10, p. 39 'How very true it is that this ridiculous distinction (between 'giving' and 'taking' in love) is a foolish invention of love!'; L.14, p. 47 'among women who paint their faces'; L.31, p. 75 dated '25 August 17—'; L.66, p. 143—the impression given on reading the footnote should be corrected by consulting the Versini ed., p. 1256, n. 2: there is no hint *here* of Valmont's wish to seduce Cécile; L.113, p. 270 'I cannot see that your return will harm this'; L.115, p. 279 'for to possess you and to lose you'; L.125, p. 297 footnote 1 'Letters 120 and 123'; L.135, p. 323 'what does it matter to him?' and 'Left to myself I thought it right'; L.140, p. 333 dated 'Paris 21 November 17—'; L.171, p. 385 'and that you no longer feel that one is made to suffer for having given way to even the most just revenge'.

(5)   A useful synopsis of the action and a sketch of the characters can be found in Faivre, pp. 17-26 and pp. 26-50 respectively. Davies has a section on characterisation, pp. 12-41. For the plot see also Belaval, pp. 35-6, and Blanc, pp. 55 ff.

(6)   See René Démoris, 'La symbolique du nom de personne dans *Les Liaisons dangereuses* ', in *Littérature* , 36 (1979), 104-119 [pp. 108-109].

(7)   Démoris, p. 110.

(8)   See Anne-Marie Jaton, *Le Corps de la liberté* , Lausanne: L'Age d'homme; Wien: Karolinger, "Romanica", 1983, p. 26.

(9)   See Versini ed., p. 1253, n. 2 to p. 127.

(10) See Versini ed., p. 1288, n. 2 to p. 176.

(11) Versini ed., pp. 757-68. See Edward C. Knox, *Patterns of Person* , Lexington, Kentucky, French Forum Publishers, 1983, p. 155, n. 13. Cf. R. Grimsley, *From Montesquieu to Laclos: Studies in the French Enlightenment* , Genève, Droz, 1974, p. 145.

(12) Hence the footnote to L.2 (F36): 'Ces mots *roué* et *rouerie* , dont heureusement la bonne compagnie commence à se défaire, étaient fort en usage à l'époque où ces Lettres ont été écrites'. But there is a hidden irony in this. Versini clarifies with an important footnote of his own:

> L'italique, souvent réservée dans *Les Liaisons* à des néologismes, étonne pour un mot qui, des roués du Régent à Valmont en passant par Marianne, semble inséparable du siècle tout entier. Malgré la note de Laclos, qui feint comme dans l'Avertissement de renvoyer les égarements dont il fait la peinture à une époque révolue, c'est bien un mot récent. [...] Il est significatif que Laclos soit responsable de l'entrée dans la langue écrite et de la fortune d'un mot qui pourrait servir d'enseigne à son roman, bien qu'il ne s'y trouve qu'une fois. (Versini ed., pp. 1172-3, n. 8)

(13) *'Les Liaisons dangereuses* , roman de l'ironie', in *Missions et démarches de la critique: Mélanges offerts au Professeur J . A . Vier* , Klincksieck, 1973, p. 655.

(14) Harry Levin, misreading the "editor"'s second footnote to L.2, gives a rather confused account of the plot preliminaries:

> Madame de Merteuil's hostility towards Cécile [...] stems from a prior attachment to the Comte de Gercourt, who had left her for a certain Intendante, who left Gercourt for Valmont, who left the Intendante for Madame de Merteuil. (*Grounds for comparison* , Boston, Harvard U.P., 1972, p. 303)

Is he inverting names when he says "who left Gercourt for Valmont" ? *Who* left the Intendante ? Is he reading 'qui' as 'que' in the phrase 'qui lui avait sacrifié le Vicomte de Valmont' (F36) (and 'sacrifié' as 'sacrifiée', presumably) ? Martin Turnell's version of events, in what Peter Gay describes—'Three stages on Love's Way', in *Encounter* , 9, 2 (1957), 8-20 [p. 14]—as his 'excellent analysis', is this:

Now Gercourt has had the misfortune, or the *maladresse*, to wound the sexual vanity of the two principal characters, the Vicomte de Valmont [does Valmont really care?] and the Marquise de Merteuil (who were themselves formerly lovers) by abandoning the Marquise for the Intendante de —, who leaves the Vicomte to become his mistress. They plan revenge... (*The Novel in France* , Peregrine, 1962, p. 64).

Turnell thus appears to make the Valmont-Merteuil relationship predate the Gercourt-Intendante de *** affair—whereas it is of course vital for the reader to realise that the chief justification for the old Valmont-Merteuil union is that it was an alliance of jilted lovers, if, that is, he is to be able to assess the Marquise's later sentimental protestations (L.131, etc.) at their true worth.

Philip Thody believes that 'une histoire de perdue' referred to by Merteuil in L.141 has the secondary punning meaning of "a story of a 'lost woman' " (*Laclos : 'Les Liaisons dangereuses'*, Edward Arnold, "Studies in French Literature", 14, 1970, p. 38). This is a distortion of the sense of the French for the sake of an (admittedly ingenious) dramatic irony.

(15)　See below my ch. on Valmont and Merteuil, n. 9.

(16)　For a summary of critical opinion see Michel Delon, *P .-A . Choderlos de Laclos : 'Les Liaisons dangereuses '*, PUF, 1986, p. 42.

(17)　Belaval, p. 59. No doubt Valmont's words 'il faut vous quitter un moment pour dissiper une ivresse qui s'augmente à chaque instant...' (L.48), as interpreted by a rather less spiritual Tourvel than is commonly thought, have given her an example to follow! Pizzorusso is not quite so explicit as Belaval:

si può ritenere che Laclos l'abbia esclusa [la lettera non datata, F494-5] per aver giudicato i temi di sensuale fervore che vi sono sviluppati poco consoni al disegno generale del carattere della Tourvel. ('La struttura delle *Liaisons dangereuses '*, in *Annali della Facoltà di Lettere e Filosofia , Cagliari* , 19 (1952), 50-88 [p. 87])

(18)　Henri Coulet, *Le Roman jusqu'à la Revolution* , Armand Colin, 1967, p. 481. See also the Versini ed., pp. 1361-2. Taking account of the variants (Versini ed., p. 1362), there are one or two strange ironic echoes of L.48 in the rejected letter: it is partly this link with L.48 (where Emilie, again, is involved) which leads me to believe that Laclos originally intended the ironic clash described, though of course there is no real way of substantiating this. A pity Laclos left no work notes.

(19) See, below, my chapter on the Valmont-Merteuil relationship, pp. 125-6.

(20) See, below, my chapter on the moral, n. 14.

(21) See Delon, p. 59; Jean Fabre's article, p. 662; Versini ed., p. 1411, n. 4.

(22) 'The Old Régime and the feminist revolution: Laclos's "De l'Education des Femmes" ', in *Yale French Studies* , 63 (1982), 139-62 [p. 161, and again, p. 162].

(23) 'Three Stages on Love's Way', p. 15.

(24) See Roger Vailland, *Laclos par lui-même* , Seuil, "Ecrivains de toujours", 1959, p. 75.

(25) Vailland, p, 72.

(26) V. Dorothy Thelander, *Laclos and the epistolary novel* , Genève, Droz, 1963, pp. 32-3. N.B., there is a misprint in the Versini ed., p. 1166, n. 1 (to p. 5 of Versini's text): read 'voir par exemple lettres [...] XLI-XLII', not 'XXXI-XXXII'.

(27) With some of the male characters in the letters or anecdotes, the capacity for sexual performance might seem a little out of the ordinary, though this is an acceptable convention of the libertine novel (see Jaton, *Le Corps de la liberté* , p. 66 and n. 88).

(28) 'Le temps et les temps dans *Les Liaisons dangereuses* ', in *Etudes françaises* , VIII, 4 (1972), 387-97 [p. 389].

(29) See also B. Duyfhuizen's article, p. 14.

(30) Tzvetan Todorov, 'Laclos et la théorie du récit', in *Tel Quel* , 27 (1966), 17-28; Maurice Roelens, 'Le texte et ses "conditions d'existence": l'exemple des *Liaisons dangereuses'*, in *Littérature* , 1 (Feb., 1971), 73-81. The novel as an auto-referential system is an idea which gives rise to some quite esoteric criticism. For a clear discussion consult Philip Stewart, *Rereadings: Eight Early French Novels,* Birmingham, Alabama, Summa Publications, 1984.

(31) Blanc, p. 70; R. Laufer, 'La structure dialectique des *Liaisons dangereuses* ', in *La Pensée* , 93 (1960), 82-90 [p. 85]; R.

Barny, 'Madame de Merteuil et la critique du libertinage', in *Dix-huitième Siècle* , 15 (1983), p. 376. Many critics comment on Merteuil's masculinity: John Pappas in 'Le moralisme des *Liaisons dangereuses* ' in *Dix-huitième Siecle* , 2 (1970), p. 286, and Versini in *Laclos et la tradition* , p. 562, for example.

(32)   Penguin Classics, 1985, pp. 48-9.

(33)   Pp. 49-50 in the Penguin Classics edition.

(34)   For further discussion of the supposed lesbianism of Merteuil consult the Versini ed., p. 1202, n. 3. Jaton very perceptively comments (*op. cit.* , pp. 47-8) that:

> ce qui est beaucoup plus 'inquiétant', dans cet épisode [L1.54-55], c'est la réponse instinctive de Cécile aux sollicitations de la Marquise. [...] Laclos semble suggérer que, chez les adolescents du moins, la sexualité n'est pas si nettement orientée que le croient les partisans de la 'Nature',

and notes that the Marquise's "masculine" preference for rather effeminate lovers is, in fact, ironic mimicry of men's propensity to turn women into sexual objects (pp. 63-4).

(35)   Alfred-Owen Aldridge, 'Essai sur les personnages des *Liaisons dangereuses* en tant que types littéraires', in *Archives des lettres modernes* , 31 (1960), 3-56 [pp. 40-41].

(36)   'Les *Liaisons dangereuses* ou le miroir ennemi', in *Revue des sciences humaines* , 153 (1974), 125-43.

(37)   See John Pappas, 'Le Moralisme des *Liaisons dangereuses* '.

(38)   Belaval, pp. 39 and 41.

(39)   Duranton, p. 129.

(40)   Coulet, p. 479.

(41)   There is no need, at this point, to rehearse objections to Vailland's late fifties Marxist analysis of the class struggle supposedly depicted in the novel. This viewpoint, no doubt developed from a meditation on Dard's ideas and from hints in Baudelaire's notes on *Les Liaisons* (v. Allem Pléiade ed. of Laclos's *Œuvres complètes* , NRF, 1943, p. 741) is no longer accepted by modern critics (see Versini ed., p. 1141; Faivre pp. 6 ff.; Davies, p. 71), though A.-M. Jaton has introduced

an important nuance into the argument (*op. cit.,* pp. 25 ff.). Conversely Michel Butor stretches the bounds of credibility when he attributes to Laclos a snobbish, almost hyper-aristocratic motive for writing (see *Répertoire II,* Editions de Minuit, 1964, pp. 150-1).

Two academics who exploit the 'Laclos and his times' approach in more recent studies are Karl Heinz Bender and Jennifer Birkett. Bender's 'L'origine sociale du malheur ou l'exclusivisme de la haute aristocratie dans *Les Liaisons dangereuses'* (*CHLR* , VII, 1-2 [1983], 53-75) is a painstaking article, but the research seems more worthwhile than some of the conclusions drawn from it (see p. 72, for example). A more sophisticated and nuanced interpretation (J. Birkett, 'Dangerous Liaisons: literary and political form in Choderlos de Laclos', in *Literature and History,* VIII, 1 [1982], 82-94) distinguishes between Rousseau, who criticises the corruption of the *ancien régime* , and Laclos, who 'depends on the order for survival; his fortunes are irrevocably implicated in that which he condemns' (p. 84), the novel itself demonstrating that ambivalence. Birkett's conclusion is:

> The ultimate political thrust of Laclos's novel is indicated by the ability of the society it depicts to absorb the outrages of individuals, and even to thrive on them. Its fabric is not weakened but strengthened by the immolation of its scapegoats; united by the threat they pose, legal and social authorities close ranks. Malraux writes: 'The reader of the *Liaisons* could have said: "Things can't go on like that"'; but in fact, the novel clearly demonstrates that such contradictions *can* endure; and in its admiration for the *apparent* scope they give to some individuals, indicates that for Laclos at least they are not, perhaps, entirely undesirable. (pp. 92-3)

But there are some sections of her article which are difficult to follow. The following, for instance:

> the stature of Valmont-Merteuil, so indisputably the centre of their social sphere, depends on the reduction of the stories of Prévan and his three mistresses, or of the Vicomtesse, whose seduction and discarding by Valmont occupy only two short letters at the very beginning of the book. (p. 87)

(42)   Emile Dard, *Le Général Choderlos de Laclos...* , Perrin, 1905, p. 32.

(43)   Versini ed., p. 703.

(44)   The testimony of Tilly, for example, is dismissed in A. & Y.
         Delmas, *A la recherche des 'Liaisons dangereuses'* , Mercure
         de France, 1964, pp. 27 ff. Versini is equally sceptical of the
         objectivity of Laclos's political interpretation of *Les Liaisons
         dangereuses* in 1791 as he is of that of the earlier letters to
         Mme Riccoboni a few days after publication of the novel: see
         Versini ed., p. 1544, n. 1 to p. 643 of Versini's text.

(45)   Seylaz's absorbing study '...(l)es mots "amour", "aimer"
         chez Mme de Merteuil et Valmont', in *RHLF* , LXXXII,
         4 (1982), 559-574 takes account of some of the most
         significant and revealing of the variants.

(46)   'Les clefs des *Liaisons dangereuses* ', in *La Revue des deux
         mondes* , 15 avril 1961, pp. 682-99.

(47)   V. Poisson, p. 80.
         It is an old problem. Do we see more merit in a Ronsard love
         sonnet, knowing that he loved a real-life woman of flesh and
         blood, to whom the poem is addressed, and was not just
         borrowing from Petrarchism ? We may be deceiving ourselves
         if we do. There need be no essential linkage between personal
         experience and good literary technique. Some of Ronsard's
         most personal-sounding, most "sincere", most technically
         accomplished poetry—*Sur la mort de Marie* , for example—
         was written to order.

(48)   Versini ed., p. 813. For other links between his
         correspondence with his wife and the novel see Versini ed., p.
         803, n. 1 (pp. 1604-1605); p. 806 'vérités de sentiment'—cf.
         L.139.

(49)   In a letter to his wife of the 28th frimaire of year IX (19
         December, 1800), Laclos wrote:

         > Je vois avec bien du plaisir qu'enfin tu te sais aimée;
         > mais tu me permettras de te dire qu'*il y a plus de dix-huit
         > ans* que tu dois en être bien sûre. (Versini ed., p. 1014,
         > my italics)

         Poisson, however, dates the start of the liaison to the winter of
         1782, i.e. five or six months *after* the publication of *Les
         Liaisons* (p. 151).

(50)   This late insertion in the text, for which see Versini ed. p. 1236
         n. 2 ('Pourquoi supposer que cette addition portée sur l'édition

ne serait pas sincère ?'), perhaps explains why Laclos cut the variant 'i' in L.110, where originally the "editor" humourlessly comments on Valmont's "profanation" of Rousseau (Versini ed., p. 1331). Perhaps at the point of publication Laclos was already beginning to have doubts about the wisdom of his ironic presentation of the sacred values of sensibility.

Compare Joan DeJean, *Literary Fortifications* , Princeton U.P., 1984, p. 223, where DeJean sees in the original variant, not irony at the expense of the Rousseauian "rédacteur ", but a possible collusion between the ironic "rédacteur" and Valmont at the expense of Rousseau. No doubt both interpretations are viable provided that we remember that Laclos did suppress the variant.

(51)   Retrospective arguments of this sort occur in Pomeau, *op. cit.* , pp. 53-4, 58-9, and 62-4.

(52)   'Laclos and Women's Education', *French Studies* , XXXVIII (1984), 144-58.

(53)   Especially as critics who ignore chronology and explain the earlier work in terms of the later cannot agree amongst themselves. The woman in *Les Liaisons dangereuses* who most closely resembles 'la femme à l'état de nature' of the *Essai sur l'éducation des femmes* is variously seen as Tourvel, or perhaps Merteuil, or perhaps again Cécile: see P. Hoffmann, 'Aspects de la condition féminine dans *Les Liaisons dangereuses* de Choderlos de Laclos', in *L'Information littéraire* , 15 (1963), 47-53 [p. 52], and compare T. Florenne, 'Figures de l'amour dans *Les Liaisons dangereuses* ', in *Littérature* , 60 (1985), 48-55 [p. 53].

Notes on 'Moral'

(1)   Henceforth F, V, and A, prefacing a number, will indicate the relevant page in the Folio, Versini, and Allem editions respectively. (Early critical assessments of *Les Liaisons* are footnoted in V, but given in full in A: hence the need to refer to two alternative editions.) I use *op. cit.* and *art. cit.* where titles have already been given in full in the introductory chapter ; many of the books and articles in question also feature in the select bibliography at the end.

For the physiological effects of novel reading, see Jaton, *op . cit* ., p. 149, n. 68. The Riccoboni correspondence is to be found in V757-68 or A710-22; the opinion of the bishop and the quotation on 'Livres de morale' in V1075 and V449 respectively; the reference to Proust in *A La Recherche du temps perdu* , "Bibliothèque de la Pléiade", III, p. 380. As for Tilly's "evidence", already mentioned in the first chapter (n. 44), consult A. & Y. Delmas *op . cit* ., pp. 27 ff. René Pomeau, in his excellent study *Laclos* (in the "Connaissance des Lettres" series) is much given to retrospective arguments: see n. 51 to the previous chapter. For a more subtle view of Laclos's "Rousseauism"—and for some interesting reactions to Versini's ideas on Laclos's moral intentions in his monumental *Laclos et la tradition* —consult John Pappas, *art . cit* . Henri Duranton, on the other hand, is more cautious. For him:

> L'œuvre s'offre donc comme le reflet amplifié de l'ironique jeu de face à face des deux préfaces qui s'annulent si parfaitement. Il faut s'y résigner. Pour découvrir une intention morale dans *Les Liaisons dangereuses* , le critique doit se munir au préalable de ce dont il a besoin avant de pénétrer dans cette auberge espagnole, ou bien, en désespoir de cause, il devra affirmer, avec Henri Coulet, que 'le livre portait sa moralité en lui-même', ce qui est assez dire qu'il n'en a pas—du moins d'explicite. (*art . cit* ., p.126)

'Cette auberge espagnole' is an allusion to Maurois's dictum 'Il en est de la lecture comme des auberges espagnoles: on n'y trouve que ce qu'on y apporte'.

(2)   Irvine Wolfarth's choice of phrase—he talks of the *'libertin* [...] pragmatism' with which the publisher in the 'Avertissement' dismisses Cécile and Mme de Tourvel—is somewhat unfortunate: see 'The irony of criticism and the criticism of irony', in *SVEC* , 120 (1974), 269-317 [p. 270].

(3)   See Baudelaire's notes on *Les Liaisons* : 'Avertissement de l'éditeur et préface de l'auteur [*sic*] (sentiments feints et dissimulés)' (A738). Nevertheless, some critics seem to take them at face value: v. Pomeau, *op . cit* ., p. 59; Angus A. Martin, 'Laclos, an unsuccessful moralist ?', in *Australian Journal of French Studies* , 1 (1964), 164-73; cf. V1169-70, notes 2 and 3.

According to Peter Gay, 'in advertising *Les Liaisons dangereuses* as a moral novel, Laclos is lying either to his reader or to himself ' (*art . cit* ., p. 15) . In fact, Laclos consciously chooses an ambiguous tone and style so as to put the reader on his guard.

(4)   'Curieuse moralité, avouons-le, qui fait de Prévan, candidat avéré à la succession de Valmont, l'objet de l'admiration attendrie de toute la bonne société' says H. Duranton, *art . cit* ., p. 125. We can easily forget that this is precisely the socially critical point Laclos is making. Pomeau's comment 'Plaisante restauration des valeurs morales, celle qui comporte l'apothéose d'un libertin ! ', *op . cit* ., p. 68, might lead us to reflect that as readers we are not so much conventionally shocked by the failure of true moral values to reassert themselves, as ironically aware of the paradox that society, while attacking hypocrisy, reinforces the double standard which breeds it.

(5)   In the preface to *Adolphe* , Constant talks of a 'société factice, qui supplée aux principes par les règles [...] et qui hait le scandale comme importun, non comme immoral, car elle accueille assez bien le vice quand le scandale ne s'y trouve pas' (quoted by S. Lotringer, 'Vice de forme', in *Critique* , 27 (1971), 195-209 [p. 199, n. 4]).

(6)   Grimm is remarkably imperceptive: for him Mme de Volanges is 'une femme dont la vie fut toujours irréprochable' (A726). Has he forgotten Merteuil's revelation about Volanges's past (L.106), or does he just not believe the Marquise?

(7)   Mme de Volanges, in her final letters to Mme de Rosemonde, may be concealing her belated discovery of the Valmont-Cécile affair with prudish hypocrisy (e.g. L.173 ?). It is indeed extraordinary if the mother has not found out about her daughter's miscarriage. Yet surely we must assume that L.173 is the naive application by Mme de Volanges of what little she has observed of her daughter to the rumours about the duel reported in L.168, in order to help her try to understand Cécile's decision to enter a convent, rather than the camouflaging of a greater crime (Valmont's relations with Cécile) beneath speculation about a lesser offence (Danceny's relationship with her daughter). After all, Mme de Volanges needs to be a naive but honest narrator for us to feel the poignancy both of her account of the Présidente's death and of the final dramatic irony of the book.

(8)   Compare 'folle illusion', 'Divinité' (F221), with 'perfections chimériques', 'Dieu' (F300) ; note the idea of self-control—admittedly to a different end— in L.81.

(9)   Cosmetics were all-important in a necessarily cosmetic society
        (see, for instance Patrick Süskind's obsessive novel *Perfume* ,
        Penguin, 1987, p. 98), and fashionable eighteenth-century
        cosmetics often produced the effect of a mask (v. A.-M. Jaton,
        op . cit ., p. 167, n. 63). But Merteuil, until her purposes are
        penetrated, wears a moral as well as a physical mask.

(10)   La Harpe, however, accuses Laclos of *invraisemblance* : 'on ne
        veut laisser à personne de pareilles preuves contre soi' (A728).

(11)   Criticism of others for these faults is an especially unreliable
        form of self-praise. Like Benjamin Franklin's children:

> Being forbid to praise themselves, they learn instead of it
> to censure others, which is only a roundabout way of
> praising themselves; for condemning the conduct of
> another, in any particular, amounts to as much as saying:
> *I am so honest, or wise, or good, or prudent, that I
> could not do or approve of such an action* . This
> fondness for ourselves, rather than malevolence to
> others, I take to be the general source of censure and
> backbiting. (To Jared Eliot, September 12th, 1751)

(12)   Yet Jennifer Birkett considers that 'Merteuil is redeemed in the
        eyes of the reader by the injustice of being scapegoated by her
        hypocritical contemporaries' (*art . cit* ., p. 89).

(13)   D.A. Coward, 'Laclos and the dénouement of the *Liaisons
        dangereuses* ', in *Eighteenth-Century Studies* , 5 (1972),
        431-49 [p. 436]; cf. Seylaz, *op . cit* ., p. 45, and Fabre, *art .
        cit* ., p. 659. It might be tempting to accept Coward's
        interpretation, if only because then Valmont's assurances in
        L.52 of 'un sentiment qui, en effet, ne finira, ne peut finir
        qu'avec ma vie' (F148) become unconsciously ironic. This is
        not ' "vous posséder ou mourir" ' (F361), but 'vous posséder
        et mourir'. Versini's suggestion that in allowing himself to be
        beaten Valmont creates for himself the 'sortie élégante d'un
        homme qui n'a pas su dominer ses contradictions, et à qui la
        Présidente ne répond pas' (V1398, n. 4) is interesting, but in
        that case is Valmont not rather over-reacting ? Versini's
        explanation, V1400, n. 2, does not seem completely
        reconcilable with his n. 2, V1392. For further indications of
        critical opinion, see below, note 35 of my chapter on Valmont
        and Merteuil.

(14)   La Harpe comments : 'il se trouve que Mme de Merteuil est
        assez insensée pour communiquer à un ami de Valmont *des
        lettres* [my italics] qui prouvent une trahison de celui-ci, mais

qui doivent en même temps la perdre elle-même, en prouvant qu'elle était complice' (A728). Accepting that '*des* lettres' may be an exaggeration, La Harpe seems to be basing his remarks on Danceny's words in L.169 ('quand on a été trahi dans son amour', F459) and thinking of the 'trahison' of L.96 ('J'écrivis à Danceny', etc., F269) which, if revealed to Danceny by Merteuil (see L.162) would be sufficient to provoke him to challenge Valmont to a duel. There is nothing in L.96 which brands Merteuil as an accomplice of the Vicomte —in the sexual betrayal of Danceny, at any rate. It is unlikely that the Marquise would show Danceny the whole of L.96. If, on the other hand, she has shown the young man L.158 (v. H. Blanc, *op . cit* ., p. 43; V1398, n. 1), how can there be any question of her being an accomplice in Valmont's treachery?

(15) In Grimm's opinion: 'Toutes les circonstances de ce dénouement, assez brusquement amenées, n'occupent guère que quatre ou cinq pages [an exaggeration: see Pomeau, p. 99]; en conscience, peut-on présumer que ce soit assez de morale pour détruire le poison répandu dans quatre volumes de séduction, où l'art de corrompre et de tromper se trouve développé avec tout le charme que peuvent lui prêter les grâces de l'esprit et de l'imagination ?' (A724). See also Seylaz, *op . cit* ., p. 131.

For a summary of critical opinion on the dénouement, see L. Versini, *Laclos et la tradition* , p. 222, n. 24.

(16) For La Harpe, however: 'Il est [...] absurde que cette femme, à qui sans doute un homme de plus ou de moins ne fait pas grand'chose, se brouille avec celui de tous qu'elle a le plus d'intérêt à ménager', A728. Contrast Seylaz, *op . cit* ., p. 40.

(17) See Lloyd Free, *art . cit* ., which, alongside the edition of Laurent Versini, the work of Seylaz, and the articles of Emita Hill and Henri Duranton, is essential reading for the student of Laclos's novel. Following up a comparison adduced by Laclos himself (V758) Lloyd Free, like La Harpe (A727), draws attention to the important example of Crébillon's Versac in *Les Egarements du cœur et de l'esprit* (1736). (For a full discussion of sources and parallels, consult L. Versini's *Laclos et la tradition.*)

The modern libertine goes one better than Valmont by implicating his mistresses in his own scheme of emotional non-involvement:

Tomas desired but feared them [women]. Needing to

create a compromise between fear and desire, he devised what he called "erotic friendship". He would tell his mistresses : the only relationship that can make both partners happy is one in which sentimentality has no place and neither partner makes any claim on the life and freedom of the other. (Milan Kundera, *The Unbearable Lightness of Being* , Faber & Faber, 1985, p.12)

Tomas's predicament is not unlike that of Valmont:

The unwritten contract of erotic friendship stipulated that Tomas should exclude all love from his life. The moment he violated that clause of the contract, his other mistresses would assume inferior status and become ripe for insurrection.(*id* ., p. 13)

In his essay on Casanova, Havelock Ellis, for his part, sees Valmont as the type of the 'cold-blooded libertine', simply; 'unscrupulously using women as the instruments of his own lust' (*Selected Essays* , J. M. Dent, 1936, p. 63).

There would be a neat symmetry and a double irony in the plot if Merteuil followed Valmont's example and betrayed *her* principles by falling in love with Danceny and failing to suppress the evidence, as Peter Gay believes she does (*art . cit* ., p. 15). But in her case the real betrayal is the loss of that self-control described in L.81's account of her 'principes' (F222), which leads her to (a) overreact to L.158 in a sudden rush of blood to the head; (b) fail to temporise (in the hope of finding a better opportunity for revenge later) by calling a truce in the 'guerre' (F432) at a point at which the two former partners have scored equally against each other (L.145 and L.158); and (c) allow Valmont to dictate the moment of her final coup, without her having thought through all the likely consequences and without having more than a fifty per cent chance of success at best: at the same time, this failure to compromise is the inevitable result of a hubris quite God-like in assuming an unerring ability to control people and events. 'Il faut tout prévoir' (L.66) is a principle which she ultimately abandons.

(18)   Suellen Diaconoff, *Eros and Power in 'Les Liaisons dangereuses'*, a Study in Evil , Genève, Droz, 1979, pp. 65 ff., has an interesting discussion of the destructive power struggle between two narcissists.

(19)   V. Seylaz, *op . cit* . , p. 51. The self-censorship which Laclos imposed on his erotic imagination is well brought out by the

MS variants suppressed in L.44 and L.76: cf. V1232, variant 'g' (to V91); and V1270, variant 'f' (to V153).

(20)   Cf. P. Thody, *op . cit .* , pp. 44 ff. and Seylaz, *op . cit.,* pp. 46-7. Detailed Racinian parallels are pursued in the Versini ed., and in Pappas, *art . cit . .* See also J. E. Flower, 'Mask and morality: Laclos's theatrical novel *Les Liaisons dangereuses* ', in *Quinquereme* , III, 2 (1980), p. 185.

(21)   In L.121, F348-9, Merteuil presents her discovery ('je / commence à être vieille!') ironically, as if inviting a rebuttal from Danceny. Compare V1181 n. 5, and V1299 n. 2 to V196. Mme de Merteuil's exclamation 'Mon Dieu, qu'une jeune femme est malheureuse!' (end of L.87) seems to support Versini's contention that she cannot be much older than Mme de Tourvel, but since the Marquise is being hypocritical about Prévan's "disgraceful" attack, is it not possible that in feigning to be in need of Mme de Volanges's mature advice, she is distorting her age, and that later, hoping for advice herself, Mme de Volanges should flatteringly continue the fiction (L.98, end)? Most readers will, rightly or wrongly, picture Merteuil as an "experienced" and therefore mature woman. Why would she claim 'je ne suis pas encore réduite à l'éducation des enfants!' (L.113, F331—a task traditionally reserved for older women) unless, underlying the comic protest, she was aware that she was older than she cared to think ? Similarly, Valmont's barely disguised insult (L.144, F409-10) would lose its point, if that were not the case.

(22)   The theft of the diamonds is perhaps not as significant as is sometimes suggested (see Michel Delon, *op . cit .* , p. 91); money is no consolation, though it does allow her to survive. At least such an attenuation of complete ruin should prevent us from talking of Laclos's urge to avenge himself remorselessly upon a character who has dangerously usurped his imagination.

(23)   See Laclos's correspondence with Mme Riccoboni, L.VII: 'Mais rappelez-vous les événements de nos jours, et vous retrouverez une foule de traits semblables dont les héros des deux sexes ne sont ou n'ont été que mieux accueillis et plus honorés' (A721)—it is just one further aspect of society's hypocrisy that it condemns on paper what it tolerates in practice. Having hinted in this exchange of letters and through the irony of the 'Avertissement de l'éditeur' (second paragraph) that *Les Liaisons* is a 'roman à clefs'—a useful device to increase the sales!—Laclos, if accused of causing scandal, can wryly point to the artificial ending of his book.

(24) William Mead, '*Les Liaisons dangereuses* and moral usefulness', *PMLA* , 75 (1960), p. 568: v. L.22, or L. 90, sixth paragraph. This is the point which Laclos no doubt wishes to emphasise, rather than the banal 'vérité importante' of the "editor" 'que toute femme qui consent à recevoir dans sa société un homme sans mœurs, finit par en devenir la victime' (F30).

(25) Mead article, *ibid* .; my italics. Ironically it is Mme de Volanges who makes the point—'Cette sensibilité si active est, sans doute, une qualité louable; mais combien tout ce qu'on voit chaque jour nous apprend à la craindre!' (L.165, F453)— without realising the implication of her words as far as her daughter is concerned (see V1283 n. 2 to V170 for the ambiguity of the adjective 'sensible' and its related noun).

(26) V. L.139, F398: 'Je ne vous ferai point le détail des faits ou des raisons qui le justifient; peut-être même l'esprit les apprécierait mal: c'est au cœur seul qu'il appartient de les sentir.' She is pardoned her weakness through the magnanimity of her final gesture in the death-bed scene (F451). Note that the Présidente does not die out of remorse at having broken her marriage vows. She dies because she hears of the death of Valmont, a second blow which, coming after his desertion of her, she is unable to withstand. Though Tourvel dies *for* love, evoking the reader's sympathy for the nobility of her self-sacrifice and affirming sentimental values in and through her death, it is also true to say that she dies *from* love, showing less ambiguously than Valmont, whose duelling "suicide" is only conjectural, how truly destructive passion can be.

(27) Cf. Clifton Cherpack, 'A new look at the *Liaisons dangereuses* ', in *Modern Language Notes* , 74 (1959), 513-21; cp. Pomeau, *op . cit* ., pp. 182-3.

(28) Cp. Beaulieu's comment: 'la publicité des ruses du crime en est peut-être plus l'instruction que le préservatif; et s'il existe des êtres aussi pervers que le vicomte de Valmont et la marquise de Merteuil, la punition que leur inflige le roman du chevalier de Laclos n'empêchera pas de les imiter, et apprendra peut-être plutôt à perfectionner leur scélératesse' (A928, n. 2).

(29) V. Seylaz, *op . cit* ., p. 101.

(30) Montjoie attributed this characteristic to Laclos himself: v. E. Dard, *Le Général Choderlos de Laclos* , p. 160.

(31) While not bringing complete ruin and destitution, the end of the book represents a total defeat for Mme de Merteuil and her plans. Some critics, however, do not agree. The conclusion of C.J. Greshoff's intuitive and discerning article 'The moral structure of *Les Liaisons dangereuses* ', in *French Review,* 37 (1964), 383-99, is this:

> Mme de Merteuil did not, for her evil actions, depend on either wealth or her looks, but solely on her mind. But this truly satanic mind, now housed in a disfigured body, remains untouched. The real Mme de Merteuil continues to live. She cannot die. She is immortal and indestructible in the same way that evil is immortal and indestructible.

It is instructive to consult Versini's strictures, V1141, and to compare V1409, n. 1, with Greshoff. See also R. Grimsley, *art . cit* ., pp. 151-2. In dismissing the idea that *Valmont* is in any way a satanic character, Grimsley possibly goes too far: Valmont's chief sin, like Satan's, was pride. Merteuil had pointed out this failing in him ('Où nous conduit pourtant la vanité!', L.145, F411) without realising that it would be her own downfall—the immoralists who, with perverse irony, draw the moral for others, are, by a supreme irony, ultimately as shortsighted as the blind or hypocritical moralisers like Volanges or Rosemonde.

(32) It is Merteuil who foresees Mme de Rosemonde's weakness on this score (L.113, F327, F328). An early, warning letter, especially coming from a less conventional figure than Mme de Volanges; or a less naive, less blind L.122, even if intercepted (v. L.110), would have made the Vicomte's task described in L.125 hard (a relative should be the first to spot play-acting). Later on, Mme de Rosemonde's ruminations (L.130) help to prolong the Présidente's suffering (see L.139).

(33) Since Laclos convicts Rosemonde (and even Tourvel) of hypocrisy, it is not quite true to say that:

> Le pessimisme social de Laclos a une limite absolue, c'est l'existence de personnes comme Mme de Tourvel et Mme de Rosemonde. Laclos peut douter de leur capacité biologique de survivre, mais il ne met aucunement en doute leur intégrité morale. (Philip Stewart, *Le Masque et la parole* , Corti , 1973, p. 194).

David Coward (in 'Laclos studies, 1968-82', in *SVEC* , 219 [1983], p. 327) argues that 'there is surely a case for a harder look at Rosemonde (who, for some critics, represents the moral centre of the book, if not L's own stoical point of view)'. No doubt I take too "hard" a view of the character—but it is sometimes necessary to redress the balance of critical opinion. My own emphasis differs as much from that of Versini (for whom 'Le rôle de Mme de Rosemonde ne fera que grandir désormais, rôle de confidente et d'autorité morale, rôle de témoin sinon de juge, lorsqu'elle survivra presque seule aux égarements de la jeunesse', V1318, n. 1 to V234, L.103) and Béatrice Didier ('Mme de Rosemonde [...] représente, dans un monde où l'intelligence est mise au service du mal, où la vertu est souvent défendue par la sottise [Mme de Volanges], la sagesse alliée à la bonté': *Les Liaisons dangereuses* , Livre de poche edition [1988], p. 596) as it does from the ideas of John Pappas (for whom 'Madame de Rosemonde est le porteur du message moral de Laclos': *art . cit..*, p. 286, and see p. 295 for Mme de Volanges). Cf. also Belaval, *op. cit* ., p. 71.

(34)   *The Novel of Worldliness* , Princeton, U.P., 1969, p. 212 (I have singled out one sentence in an excellent study).

(35)   Cf. L. Versini, *'Les Liaisons dangereuses* 1982', in *L'Information littéraire* , 34 (1982), 23-5 [p. 25]: 'Le dénouement semble devoir se lire sur deux registres.'

Notes on 'Irony'

(1)   For a historical survey of irony in Classical times see J.A.K. Thomson, *Irony: An Historical Introduction* , London, George Allen & Unwin Ltd., 1926. A summary of the development of irony and its meaning from Plato to modern times (based on the work of G.G. Sedgewick) may be found in *The word Irony and its Context, 1500-1755* , by Norman Knox (Durham, N.C.: Duke U.P., 1961), pp. 3-23. D.C. Muecke's *The Compass of Irony* , Methuen, 1969, is a taxonomy of great precision; Wayne C. Booth's *A Rhetoric of Irony* , Chicago, University Press, 1974, includes an interesting bibliography; and D.J. Enright's *The Alluring Problem: An Essay on Irony* , Oxford, University Press, 1986, offers an engagingly entertaining approach to the subject. The most celebrated French study of Laclosian irony is the article of Jean Fabre cited in the bibliography.

(2)   *The Rhetoric of Fiction* , second edition, University of Chicago

Press, 1983, ch. 10, p. 304.

(3)   See for example: L.66: 'Voilà bien les hommes! tous également scélérats dans leurs projets, ce qu'ils mettent de faiblesse dans l'exécution, ils l'appellent probité'; L.110: 'celle qui ne respecte pas sa mère, ne se respectera pas elle-même: vérité morale que je crois si utile que j'ai été bien aise de fournir un exemple à l'appui du précepte'; L.125: 'lisez donc, et voyez à quoi s'expose la sagesse, en essayant de secourir la folie'.

(4)   Compare, for example, L.104 with the last paragraphs of L.106.

(5)   See the biblical parody in L.63, F168; or L.85: 'Le Diable me tentait. [...] Je m'acheminais ainsi à ma perte' (F246).

(6)   Some examples: 'Oh! l'on peut se brouiller avec celui-là [Danceny]; les raccommodements ne sont pas dangereux (L.54: yet see Ll. 158-9, 162-3, 168!); 'il faut tout prévoir' (L.66); 'ce sont les bons nageurs qui se noient' (L.76); 'Il faut vaincre ou périr' (L.81); 'Où nous conduit pourtant la vanité!' (L.145: for the answer, see L.159 and its aftermath).

(7)   See V1174, n. 10. Cf. Valmont's use of the word 'honnêteté' in L.71 (F187) and Versini's comment, V1263, n. 7.

(8)   See Pomeau, *op . cit* ., pp. 105-106. Pomeau cites one title, Vulson de la Colombière's *Le Vrai théâtre d'honneur et de chevalerie* (1748) as an example of 'la vogue du genre troubadour'. For further documentation of primary and secondary sources for the eighteenth century's revival of interest in the medieval genre, consult Lloyd Free, 'Laclos and the myth of courtly love', pp. 202-203 in *SVEC* , 148 (1976), 201-23.

Pomeau concludes: 'La référence au vocabulaire chevaleresque souligne le caractère aristocratique du libertinage. Par leurs prouesses les libertins constituent une sorte de chevalerie moderne' (*op . cit* ., p. 106). Lloyd Free's article, despite being mangled by the printers, demonstrates how antithetical are the values of libertinism and courtly love, thus accounting for the attraction of Valmont and Merteuil to this particular source of irony. By an irony not of his own volition, however, the Vicomte's parody of courtly love (initially employed as a seduction technique) comes dangerously close to the real thing once the Présidente has succumbed to his wishes.

(9) Laclos seems to delight in exploding the sentimental cliché—not only Rousseauesque (L.11, F57; L.22, F77), but also of a more traditional hue. Here are some examples:
(i) the ironically banal use of the harp as the mediator of the lovers' sensibilities (L.16 and L.18);
(ii) Valmont's *désabusé* conclusion 'et puis, qu'on dise que l'amour rend ingénieux! il abrutit au contraire ceux qu'il domine' (L.133, F384)—a reversal of a favourite Renaissance commonplace of love;
(iii) Valmont's occasional ironical deployment of a hackneyed precious image from earlier love poetry, such as 'je résistai à un petit nuage d'humeur qui obscurcit, toute la soirée, cette figure céleste' (L.21, F74), or 'Ne savez-vous pas que la seule volupté a le droit de détacher le bandeau de l'amour ?' (L.6, F44)—a cliché from Renaissance emblem books and elsewhere, but undercut with libertine worldweariness; or 'Cécile ignore que les flèches de l'Amour, comme la lance d'Achille, portent avec elles le remède aux blessures qu'elles font' (L.99, F280);
(iv) the Présidente's imagery in L.56 (F154-5), where the very banality of a literary commonplace (Lucretius, II, 1 and 2) perhaps seems a measure of the weakness of her self-defence.

(10) *Time* , 14 September 1953. For a discussion of religious vocabulary in *Les Liaisons* see Didier's preface to the 1988 Livre de Poche edition.

(11) 'Alcanter de Brahm' (i.e. Marcel Bernhardt) suggested in *L'Ostensoir des ironies* (1899) that a special punctuation mark, 'le petit signe flagellateur', should be used to indicate the presence of irony. Muecke calls this idea 'preposterous' (*op. cit* ., p. 56), but the readers of *Les Liaisons dangereuses* might not necessarily always agree with him.

(12) For other examples of private irony, see my chapter on the Valmont-Merteuil relationship, pp. 114 and 118.

(13) See V1190, n. 4.

(14) Fabre, *art . cit* ., p. 659. Apparently it is paradoxical and inconsistent to accept the idea of Valmont's genuine love and reject the theory of his suicide for love. However, see below the Valmont-Merteuil chapter, n. 35.

(15) See P. Thody, *op . cit* ., p. 25.

(16) Whether we say that characters intent on controlling and

eliminating feeling are finally brought down by emotion or by *lack* of emotion, in either case the irony is appropriate.

(17) In his revision of the novel, Laclos preferred to stand by dramatic irony as a means of revealing Cécile's naivety, and to eschew more obvious touches: see L.95, MS variant, F491.

(18) Nevertheless, a stronger moral irony is that Merteuil the hypocrite becomes the victim of a hypocritical society. For the final dramatic ironies which involve Mme de Volanges, see the end of my chapter on the moral, where I argue that Volanges, in this case, is blind but not hypocritical.

(19) Anselme is a *feuillant* : a member of the Cistercian order reformed by St. Bernard (whose views on the weakness of women, while not quite as picturesque as those of Odo of Cluny, were not noticeably restrained). Laclos, through dramatic irony, makes the gullibility of an individual priest totally risible, but because he sees religion as a source of illusion (v. Roger Vailland, *op . cit .*, p. 175) this hardly proves that he "really sympathises" with the schemes of his libertines, if his plan is to wield irony ultimately to force us to see the folly of their pretensions.

(20) 'L'honnête jeune homme! ', comments Jean Fabre sarcastically (*art. cit .*, p. 658) .

(21) Marion Boyars, 1965.

Notes on 'Structure'

(1) See Arnaldo Pizzorusso, *art . cit .*, 'La struttura delle *Liaisons dangereuses* ', pp. 82 ff.

(2) With regard to the protagonists' mutual revenge at the end of the novel, Merteuil's 'alternative' as early as the beginning of L.2 (F35-6) already anticipates the later polarisation of the arch-rivals' positions, and the Marquise's evocative response ('Hé bien! la guerre') to the Vicomte's ultimatum (L.153); Valmont's 'conquérir est notre destin' (L.4, F39) and Merteuil's 'Il faut vaincre ou périr' (L.81, F230) ultimately leave no room for compromise.

(3)   Cf. Belaval, *op . cit .*, p. 51, and Versini *Le Roman épistolaire,* p. 155.

(4)   V. Thelander, *op . cit .*, p. 59.

(5)   'la femme dans le grand corridor, [...] le mari d'un côté et l'Amant de l'autre', with Valmont 'vis-à-vis' (F187).

(6)   As Versini observes:

> A la "distraction" que Valmont trouve en compagnie de Cécile, elle [Merteuil] répond par une séduction symétrique qui opère un chassé-croisé par rapport au temps où Valmont était l'instituteur de Danceny et la Marquise, l'institutrice de Cécile. (V1338, n. 3 to V264)

(7)   See Thelander, *op . cit .*, p. 62.

(8)   Taking into account the date when Merteuil returns to Paris (see L. 146), and the usual incubation period of between seven and twenty-one days before the fever (L.175) declares itself in the first stages of the disease, it is equally *vraisemblable* that Merteuil could have become infected either shortly before, or shortly after, leaving the country.

(9)   Before Danceny is distracted, his words in L.116 'Quel bonheur [...] de sentir [...] qu'en m'occupant du bonheur de l'une, je travaillerais également à celui de l'autre' [sc. the happiness of Cécile and Merteuil] (F339) make him resemble Valmont whose attentions are shared by two different women.

(10)   Perhaps that could also be said of Valmont himself. In the Marquise's view, he is really no more than her sexual automaton, pleasuring a 'machine à plaisir' (F308).

(11)   It is Mme de Volanges who points this out: 'D'abord Mme de Merteuil, en effet très estimable, n'a peut-être d'autre défaut que trop de confiance en ses forces' (L.32). Ironically what Volanges says is much truer than she realises. She has superficially observed Merteuil resisting the advances of the admiring rake Valmont (see L.9, F51), when in fact they had long been lovers in private. It is Merteuil's over-confidence in the measures she takes to fend off Valmont after the seduction of Tourvel, and sidestep the agreement of L.20, which leads to her downfall.

(12)   Cf. Seylaz, *op . cit .*, p. 35.

(13)   See also L.25, F85.

(14)   Valmont's device in L.110 is already prefigured by his feint of illness in L.40 (*suite*), F123.

(15)   V. Seylaz, *op . cit* ., p. 36.

(16)   This latter point regarding Valmont would seem to be borne out by the repetition of 'mener comme un enfant' in L.96, F271: compare L.81, F220—the only other time this phrase appears. (The Vicomte's memory is conveniently defective, and the wrong attribution is deliberate.) For a possible ironic similarity between Danceny's love letters to Cécile (L.31) and to the Marquise (L.150, L.148) see V1214, n. 2, referring to V64.

(17)   For Gide 'la débauche commence où commence à se dissocier de l'amour le plaisir', *Œuvres complètes* , Vol. VII (Paris: Gallimard, n. d.), p. 453. Quoted by C. J. Greshoff, *art . cit* ., p. 387, n. 7.

(18)   See V1346, n. 2, where Versini, commenting on Merteuil's L.121 to Danceny, says:

> Mme de Merteuil's s'inspire-t-elle des lettres de Mme de Tourvel à Valmont qui les lui communique, pour jouer le personnage de l'honnête femme? Elle réclame comme elle de ne pas être confondue avec les femmes méprisables (lettres XXVI [..]; XLI [...]), et reprend deux de ses leitmotive en offrant sa franchise et son amitié (cf. lettre LXVII).

(19)   Cf. Seylaz, *op . cit* ., p. 37.

(20)   *Op . cit* ., pp. 55-6, my italics.

(21)   Cf. Philip Stewart, *Rereadings: Eight Early French Novels* , p. 258, n. 28.

(22)   V. Malraux's preface to the Folio edition, pp. 17-18, and H. Blanc, *op . cit* ., p. 22, etc.

(23)   The critics who employ the dance metaphor and talk of quadrilles forget that a quadrille is a dance for *four* couples, and is in *five* parts (not four). The chess comparison is not much of an improvement since it ignores the rules of the game. At least it is true that Valmont appears to think he can take his "pieces" more than once...

Notes on 'Valmont and Merteuil'

(1) H. Duranton, *art . cit* ., p. 131.

(2) Cf. Dominique Aury, 'La révolte de Madame de Merteuil', in *Les Cahiers de la Pléiade* , XII (1951), pp. 96, 100, 101; Georges Daniel, *Fatalité du secret et fatalité du bavardage au XVIIIe siècle* , A.-G. Nizet, 1966, pp. 41, 53, 57, 75, etc.; Pappas, *art . cit* ., pp. 273, 275.

(3) Cf. Madeleine Therrien, *'Les Liaisons dangereuses'* : *une interprétation psychologique* , S.E.D.E.S., 1973, p. 186.

(4) Cp. Therrien, *op. cit* ., p. 187, pp. 189-90; Lloyd Free, 'Crébillon fils, Laclos, and the code of the libertine', p. 38; and p. 36 of Lloyd Free's *Laclos: Critical approaches to 'Les Liaisons dangereuses'* , Madrid, 1978. Versini, in *Laclos et la tradition* , sometimes gives the impression that Merteuil has some residual feeling for Valmont (p. 220; pp. 608-9), though his views seem to have been revised: compare V1366, n. 1 to V307.

(5) Let us not forget that in his correspondence with Mme de Riccoboni, Laclos himself described Merteuil as 'un cœur incapable d'amour' (V762).

(6) Cf. R. Laufer, *art . cit* ., in *La Pensée* , 1960, p. 83: 'Lorsque l'action commence, la marquise et le vicomte se sont *depuis peu* détachés après avoir éprouvé leurs forces' (my italics).

(7) The 'mission d'amour' is a rationalisation or *reductio ad absurdum* of Valmont's capacity for infidelity.

(8) Contrast Laufer, *art . cit* ., pp. 83-4. Contrast Seylaz's article in *RHLF* , LXXXII, 4 (1982), p. 572. The excision from L.15 of the phrase noted by Seylaz 'Laissez-moi l'espoir de retrouver ces moments où nous savions fixer le bonheur [...] jaloux' (V1195, variant 'd' to V36) possibly confirms that Valmont is merely feigning jealousy and agrees with my interpretation below (main text) of a sentence of F63 as parody.

(9) L.31 includes the tell-tale phrase about the 'secrets' that Mme de Merteuil has to convey to Cécile's mother, and L.32 shows signs of being scripted by the Marquise: see 'Mais ni Mme de Merteuil elle-même , ni aucune autre femme, n'oserait sans

doute aller s'enfermer à la campagne, presque en tête à tête avec un tel homme' (F98). Merteuil thinks she is killing two birds with one stone since as well as influencing Mme de Volanges, and through her the Présidente, against Valmont, the confidential talk with Mme de Volanges provides her with an alibi, thus throwing Cécile and Danceny together without any supervision: cf. L.38 'Je lui [sc. à Cécile] ai permis d'écrire et de dire *j'aime* ; et *le jour même* , sans qu'elle s'en doutât, je lui ai *ménagé* un tête-à-tête avec son Danceny', F113 (my italics in the last two cases); note the dating of L.30 and L.31 (F95 'hier! [...] secrets'). In L.63, Merteuil's choice of phrase is perhaps an unconscious betrayal of her earlier intervention: 'je lui fis confidence [sc. à Mme de Volanges] que je me croyais sûre qu'il existait entre sa fille et Danceny une liaison dangereuse. Cette femme, si clairvoyante contre vous...' This could suggest Merteuil knows that Mme de Volanges had used the phrase 'liaison dangereuse' in her warnings to the Présidente against Valmont. The text therefore gives support to Philip Thody's theory:

> Does Madame de Merteuil carry her hostility towards Valmont to the extent of encouraging Madame de Volanges to warn La Présidente against him ? Laclos does no more than hint, but Madame de Merteuil is suspiciously friendly with Madame de Volanges in the first part of the novel and Madame de Volanges suspiciously well-informed about Valmont's earlier career. (*op . cit* ., p. 32)

However Thody's conclusion is not necessarily the only one:

> If Madame de Merteuil is behaving in this way, then it may mean either that she is more jealous of Valmont than she dare admit even to herself, or that she is actually in love with him herself and prepared to use every means to keep him away from a person whom she has already identified as her only really dangerous rival. (*ibid* .)

Merteuil would still employ these tactics whether she was passionately jealous of Mme de Tourvel, merely irritated at the latter's hold over Valmont, or jealous of Gercourt and his coming married happiness (Valmont getting nowhere with the Présidente might pick up Cécile on the rebound). Some might even say that the motivation for Merteuil's intervention at this point rather resembles the reasons she gives for putting obstacles in Danceny's path later (L.63, F167).

(10)   For Madelyn Gutwirth:

>   That there is in fact little love in him for her, except at the
>   moment of her surrender, is a point often lost sight of
>   by sentimentalists. Even at this juncture it must be asked
>   if it is not his victory that he loves as much if not more
>   than Mme de Tourvel. ('Laclos and "le sexe": the rack of
>   ambivalence', *SVEC* , 189 (1980), 247-96 [quotation
>   taken from p. 276])

(11)   Unless (but this hardly seems the tone!) there is a touch of
fatalism about Valmont's talk of swearing 'un amour éternel;
et, il faut tout avouer, je pensais ce que je disais' (F366) when
followed by the quotation from the old love letter to Merteuil
'adieu, mon Ange! ', etc.—a juxtaposition which is meant to
suggest "our love did not last, so why should my love for
Tourvel ?"

(12)   From Valmont's point of view what must really annoy Merteuil
is that he should so casually request his 'récompense' (F366)
although he does not want her at all, since he loves Tourvel.

(13)   It is hard to see how he would think it credible to argue 'de ce
que l'esprit est occupé s'ensuit-il que le cœur soit esclave ?'
(F384) when only a few pages earlier in L.125 he had been
implying that the seduction of the Présidente led to much more
than the *intellectual* satisfaction of conquest.

(14)   The juxtaposition of Ll.132 and 133 suggests Valmont's
implausibility more strongly and more immediately than it does
the Présidente's naivety, for 'L'observateur le plus pénétrant de
l'amour de Valmont pour Mme de Tourvel ce n'est pas
Valmont [...] c'est même la Présidente (CXXXII)'—Belaval,
op. cit., p. 53.

(15)   Perhaps Valmont is projecting the undoubted evidence of his
love for Tourvel at Merteuil, the repository of his libertine
conscience, but also the woman he wrongly assumes loves
him, (a) because it amuses him to see her suffering from the
same malady as himself, and (b) so that he can dismiss her
judgements as clouded by jealousy, and thus live without
qualms with his love for one brief moment longer.

(16)   The change from 'Dans le temps où nous étions uniquement
occupés l'un de l'autre' to 'Dans le temps où nous nous
aimions, car je crois que c'était de l'amour, j'étais heureuse; et
vous, Vicomte ?...' (V1366 , variant 'a' to V307) is by no

means incontrovertible evidence of Merteuil's love. It is equally likely that Merteuil's sentimental appeal to Valmont is being strengthened to emphasise the deception whereby she entices him foolishly to make a unilateral sacrifice.

(17)   At the end of L.131, Merteuil, in argument, has recourse to love 'non pour le ressentir à la vérité, mais pour l'inspirer et le feindre' (cf. L.81, F225).

(18)   Merteuil's complaints when Valmont behaves uxoriously (L.152) put all this play-acting into proper perspective.

(19)   Moreover it is unnecessary to emphasise a contradiction between that classification and Valmont's enthusiasm on F385.

(20)   Of the various interpretations of L.134 offered by Coulet, *op* . *cit.* , p. 480, his first hypothesis seems best.

(21)   See the end of L.129, and compare Versini's version: 'La Marquise doit penser à l'aigreur de la lettre V [rather a big jump backwards for the reader, surely ?] [...] qui n'a fait que confirmer Valmont dans son idolâtrie' (V1370, n. 1 to V313).

(22)   Valmont is accordingly somewhat obtuse in pretending that sensual indulgence with Emilie disproves his sentimental attachment to Mme de Tourvel (L.138).

(23)   Versini dates Merteuil's interest in Danceny, and her notion of involving Valmont, unbeknown to him, in her plans to seduce the young man, as early as L.38: see V1226, n. 4 to V78. For Roger Barny, it is L.63 which marks the starting point of her arrangements for a liaison with Danceny ('Madame de Merteuil et la critique du libertinage', in *Dix-huitième Siècle* , 15 [1983], p. 371).

(24)   These fears can be traced back and attributed particularly to the hubris of L.99 (cf. 'ils n'auront plus qu'à admirer et applaudir', F279) being so swiftly followed by the disappointment of L.100.

(25)   Versini declares that Valmont's plan is 'de se voir soumis les sens en Cécile, la tête en Mme de Merteuil et le cœur en Mme de Tourvel' (V1364, n. 1 to V303). Unfortunately he does not explain how Valmont thinks he can subdue a woman of the head with arguments of the heart, or why he should consider it necessary to do so.

(26)   She is confirming her emotional weakness, while giving him

the means to prove his strength.

(27)   No support can be given, therefore, to Aldridge's analysis, *art. cit.*, p. 39, which fails to take account of Merteuil's manipulation and Valmont's shame.

(28)   Cp. M. Therrien, *op . cit .*, p. 165. As Constant wrote in the preface to the third edition of *Adolphe* : 'nous sommes des créatures tellement mobiles que les sentiments que nous feignons, nous finissons par les éprouver' (quoted in Delmas, *op . cit .*, p. 45). Tristan Florenne alights on L.36 ('Alors je connus l'amour') to locate much earlier the point at which Valmont becomes trapped by the feelings which he at first only pretended to experience (*art . cit .*, p. 50).

(29)   *Art . cit .*, p. 130.

(30)   Cf. Lloyd Free, 'Crébillon fils, Laclos, and the code of the libertine', p. 36.

(31)   R. Pomeau, *op . cit .*, p. 132. Cf. Therrien, *op . cit .*, p. 177.

(32)   Cp. R. Lemieux, 'Valmont, libertin amoureux ou homme à projet ?', in *Romance Notes* , 20, 3 (1980), 349-54 [p. 353]. Lemieux draws no conclusions from the fact that Valmont's original letter was cut, and his article, though interesting, is based on a somewhat partial and selective reading of the text.

(33)   However Laclos himself has used the device of the "rédacteur" to justify the removal of F493-4, thus *reducing* the number of possible ambiguities from two to one, while forcing the reader, even so, to be conscious that it is the reader himself who, in the final outcome, must determine the interpretation of Valmont's emotions.

(34)   Thody, *op . cit .*, p. 14.

(35)   Seylaz, *art . cit .*, pp. 571-2. See also Lloyd Free, 'Laclos and the myth of courtly love', p. 213.

The emphasis of Seylaz's remark differs from that of Thody by suggesting that Valmont's example of his own emotional commitment to Tourvel is put forward by him as a model for Danceny to follow, but both critics agree on the essential point of sincerity.

Does it naturally follow that Valmont, in compensation for what he now recognises as his unforgivable desertion of

Tourvel, should switch from one great passion to what Freud saw as another comparable one: suicide ?—see A. Alvarez, *The Savage God* (Penguin, 1983), p. 144. Is Valmont's despair really likely to make him fail to defend himself against a Merteuil stand-in in a life-and-death duel—a battle for which, some say, all his love "battles" have been mere substitutes ? (see my chapter on Moral, n. 13) One of the implications of Seylaz's formula 'un aveu calculé mais sincère' is that the Vicomte is capable of simultaneously feeling love for Tourvel (and therefore also despair, L.154) and a desire for revenge on Merteuil. Rather than excluding each other, love and vengeance, in Valmont's case, no doubt go hand in hand. Is it unreasonable of the reader to conclude that, far from committing suicide, Valmont would do his utmost to win the duel and get his own back on Merteuil because she had forced him to betray Tourvel ? Immediately after the duel, Danceny is discovered weeping (L.163). Georges Daniel comments:

> ...en raccompagnant son adversaire mortellement blessé, Danceny pleurait avant même que celui-ci lui ait dévoilé les intrigues de Mme de Merteuil et rejeté sur elle la responsabilité de leur commun malheur. Or quelle pourrait être la cause du pardon dont témoignent ces larmes, sinon le repentir du scélérat manifesté par son refus de se défendre ? (*op . cit* ., p. 89)

But Danceny's tears could be quite simply tears of dispelled tension and relief—and self-permitted sympathy. Now that honour is satisfied he can afford to regret the suffering he has so obviously caused ('tout baigné dans son sang', F447). There is a world of difference between saying that Valmont seals his own fate by writing L.96 (see L.162), and saying that in the duel he commits suicide—despite the suggestion of one critic (Peter V. Conroy Jr., *Intimate, Intrusive, and Triumphant Readers in the 'Liaisons dangereuses'* , Amsterdam, 1987, p. 48, and note 12, p. 128). Roger Barny, *art . cit* ., p. 385, believes that in drafting the break-off letter for Valmont in L.141, Merteuil identifies herself with its ultimate addressee and commits a form of suicide, while Todorov says of the rivals' mutual betrayal of trust (see L.162, L.163, F447, and L.168, F456) 'Le roman se termine par une sorte de double suicide, chacun d'eux rendant publiques les lettres de son adversaire et causant ainsi sa ruine, morale ou physique' (*Littérature et signification* [Larousse, 1967,] p. 48). (Todorov is neatly taken to task for his terminology by Philip Stewart in his admirable *Rereadings: Eight Early French Novels* , p. 255, n. 8).

Notes on 'Feminism and Film'

(1) Anne-Marie Jaton, 'Libertinage féminin, libertinage dangereux' in *Laclos et le libertinage 1782-1982: Actes du colloque du bicentaire des 'Liaisons dangereuses'* (PUF, 1983), pp. 151-62 [p. 153].

(2) *Ibid*.

(3) *Id* ., p. 154. See L.56, F155: 'elles ont tout perdu jusqu'à l'estime de celui à qui elles ont tout sacrifié'; or L.96, F268: 'Ah! le temps ne viendra que trop tôt, où, dégradée par sa chute, elle ne sera plus pour moi qu'une femme ordinaire'. Cf. the last paragraph of L.136.

(4) A.-M. Jaton, *art. cit.*, pp. 154-7.

(5) Dominique Aury, *art . cit* ., p. 97.

(6) *Id* ., p. 98.

(7) Jaton, *art . cit* ., p. 158.

(8) *Ibid* .

(9) See endnote 5 of my previous chapter.

(10) Cp. Paul Hoffmann, 'Aspects de la condition féminine dans *Les Liaisons dangereuses* de Choderlos de Laclos', in *L'Information littéraire*, 15 (1963), 47-53.

(11) V. Shirley Jones, 'Literary and Philosophical Elements in *Les Liaisons dangereuses* : The Case of Merteuil', in *French Studies* , XXXVIII (April 1984), 159-69 [p. 163].

(12) Anne-Marie Jaton, '*Les Liaisons dangereuses* : une odyssée de la conscience sexuée', in *Saggi e richerche di letteratura francese* , 16 (1977), 299-350 [p. 320].

(13) R. Barny, however, sees more than mere polemical expediency in Merteuil's criticism of the libertine ethic (*art . cit* ., pp. 384, 386, 387).

(14) V. Jones, *art . cit* ., p. 165.

(15)   V. Jurgen von Stackelberg, 'Le féminisme de Laclos', in *Thèmes et Figures du siècle des lumières. Mélanges offerts à R. Mortier* (Genève, 1980), pp. 271-84 [pp. 273 ff.].

(16)   Cf. M. Gutwirth, *art . cit* ., p. 265. For a fuller discussion of the feminist aspects of the novel than we have time for in this brief outline, the reader is recommended to consult the excellent study of Anne-Marie Jaton, *Le Corps de la liberté* , especially the conclusion, pp. 151-7.

(17)   *Film* , I, 1 (April 1989), 23.

Notes on Conclusion

(1)   See V1241-2.

(2)   It is because Tourvel has already foreseen the moral contempt of the seducer for his victim that she is so devastated when he conforms to the pattern. Compare L.56, where she talks of the women he has seduced:

> ...sont-elles donc si méprisables? Ah! sans doute, puisqu'elles ont trahi leurs devoirs pour se livrer à un amour criminel. De ce moment, elles ont tout perdu, jusqu'à l'estime de celui à qui elles ont tout sacrifié (F155),

with L.141:

> 'Si, par exemple, j'ai eu juste autant d'amour que toi de vertu, et c'est sûrement beaucoup dire, il n'est pas étonnant que l'un ait fini en même temps que l'autre.' (F404)

(3)   See Jean Dagen, 'D'une logique de l'écriture: *Les Liaisons dangereuses* ', in *Littératures* (Toulouse), 4 (1981), 33-50 [p. 48].

Select Bibliography

The critical bibliography of *Les Liaisons dangereuses* is immense. The following is a selection from those books and articles which the student of Laclos will find most useful. Unless otherwise indicated, the place of publication is Paris.

BIBLIOGRAPHICAL STUDIES

David Coward   'Laclos Studies, 1968-1982', in *Studies on Voltaire and the Eighteenth Century* , 219, Oxford, 1983, pp. 289-328.

Michel Delon   *Vide infra* for title, "Bibliographie en langue française", pp. 122-8.

C.V. Michael   *Choderlos de Laclos The Man, His Works, and his Critics An Annotated Bibliography* , New York and London, "Garland Reference Library of the Humanities", 1982.

EDITIONS

Maurice Allem   Laclos: *Œuvres complètes* . NRF , "Bibliothèque de la Pléiade", 1943.

René Pomeau   *Les Liaisons dangereuses* . Imprimerie nationale, "Lettres françaises", 1981.

Laurent Versini   Laclos: *Œuvres complètes* . NRF Gallimard, "Bibliothèque de la Pléiade", 1979.

CRITICAL WORKS

Yvon Belaval   *Choderlos de Laclos.* Seghers, "Ecrivains d'hier et d'aujourd'hui", no. 40, 1972.

Henri Blanc   *'Les Liaisons dangereuses' de Choderlos de Laclos* . Hachette, "Poche critique", 1972.

Peter Brooks   *The Novel of Worldliness* . Princeton, U.P., 1969 [pp. 172-218].

Henri Coulet   *Le Roman jusqu'à la Révolution.* Armand Colin, 1967.

Georges Daniel   *Fatalité du secret et fatalité du bavardage au XVIIIe siècle* . A.-G. Nizet, 1966.

Simon Davies   *Laclos: 'Les Liaisons dangereuses '.* London, Grant & Cutler Ltd., "Critical Guides to French Texts", 68, 1987.

A. and Y. Delmas   *A la Recherche des 'Liaisons dangereuses'* . Mercure de France, 1964.

Michel Delon   *P.-A. Choderlos de Laclos: 'Les Liaisons dangereuses '.* PUF, "Etudes littéraires", 1986.

Suellen Diaconoff   *Eros and Power in 'Les Liaisons dangereuses' : A Study in Evil* . Genève, Droz, 1979.

Jean-Luc Faivre   *'Les Liaisons dangereuses': Laclos* . Hatier, "Profil d'une œuvre", 1973.

Lloyd Free (ed.)   *Laclos: Critical approaches to 'Les Liaisons dangereuses '.* Madrid, Porrúa Turanzas, "Studia Humanitatis", 1978.

Anne-Marie Jaton   *Le Corps de la liberté* . Lausanne: L'Age d'homme; Wien: Karolinger, "Romanica", 1983.

Vivienne Mylne	*The Eighteenth-Century French Novel: Techniques of Illusion* . Manchester, U.P., 1965.
Georges Poisson	*Choderlos de Laclos ou l'obstination* . Grasset, 1985.
René Pomeau	*Laclos* . Hatier, "Connaissance des Lettres, 1975.
	Laclos et le libertinage 1782-1982: Actes du colloque du bicentaire des Liaisons dangereuses, PUF, 'Publications du centre d'études du roman et du romanesque Université de Picardie', 1983 (preface by R. Pomeau).
Georges Poulet	*Etudes sur le temps humain, II, La Distance intérieure* . Plon, 1952.
Jean Rousset	*Forme et signification* , José Corti, 1962.
Jean-Luc Seylaz	*'Les Liaisons dangereuses' et la création romanesque chez Laclos* . Genève: Droz; Paris: Minard, 1958.
Philip Stewart,	*Rereadings: Eight Early French Novels* . Birmingham, Alabama, Summa Publications, 1984.
Madeleine Therrien	*'Les Liaisons dangereuses': une interprétation psychologique* . SEDES, 1973.
Philip Thody	*Laclos: 'Les Liaisons dangereuses'* . London, Edward Arnold, "Studies in French Literature", 14 , 1970.
Roger Vailland	*Laclos par lui-même* . Seuil, "Ecrivains de toujours", 1959.
Laurent Versini	*Laclos et la tradition* . Klincksieck, 1968.

ARTICLES

Dominique Aury

'La Révolte de Madame de Merteuil', in *Les Cahiers de la Pléiade* , XII (1951), 91-101.

Roger Barny

'Madame de Merteuil et la critique du libertinage', in *Dix-huitième Siècle* , 15 (1983), 369-88.

Jennifer Birkett

'Dangerous Liaisons: Literary and Political Form in Choderlos de Laclos', in *Literature and History* , 8, 1 (1982), 82-94.

G. Castel-Çagarriga

'Les Clefs des "Liaisons dangereuses" ', in *La Revue des deux mondes* , 15 avril 1961, pp. 682-99.

Clifton Cherpack

'A New Look at the *Liaisons dangereuses'*, in *Modern Language Notes,* 74 (1959), 513-21.

Henri Duranton

'*Les Liaisons dangereuses* ou le miroir ennemi', in *Revue des sciences humaines,* 153 (1974), 125-43.

Jean Fabre

'*Les Liaisons dangereuses* , roman de l'ironie', in *Missions et démarches de la critique; Mélanges offerts au Professeur J.A. Vier* . Klincksieck, 1973, pp. 651-72.

J.E. Flower

'Mask and Morality: Laclos's Theatrical Novel *Les Liaisons dangereuses'*, in *Quinquereme* , III, 2 (1980), 183-92.

Lloyd Free

'Crébillon fils, Laclos, and the Code of the Libertine', in *Eighteenth-Century Life* , I (1974), 36-40.

Hugo Friedrich

'Immoralismus und Tugendideal in den *Liaisons dangereuses* ', in *Romanische Forschungen* , XLIX (1935), 317-42.

Helena Goscilo — 'Tolstoy, Laclos, and the Libertine', in *The Modern Language Review*, LXXXI (1986), 398-414.

C.J. Greshoff — 'The Moral Structure of *Les Liaisons dangereuses*', in *French Review*, 37 (1964), 383-99.

Ronald Grimsley — 'Don Juanism in *Les Liaisons dangereuses*', an article reprinted in his book *From Montesquieu to Laclos: Studies on the French Enlightenment*, Genève, Droz, 1974, pp. 145-59.

Emita B. Hill — 'Man and Mask. The Art of the Actor in *Les Liaisons dangereuses*', in *Romanic Review*, 63 (1972), 111-24.

E. Sculley Hudon — 'Love and Myth in *Les Liaisons dangereuses*', in *Yale French Studies*, 11 (1953), 25-38.

Shirley Jones — 'Literary and Philosophical Elements in *Les Liaisons dangereuses*: the Case of Merteuil', in *French Studies*, XXXVIII (1984), 159-69.

Haydn Mason — '*Les Liaisons dangereuses*: A Tract for the Times?', an article reprinted in his book *French Writers and their Society (1715-1800)*, London, Macmillan, 1982, pp. 197-208.

William Mead — '*Les Liaisons dangereuses* and Moral Usefulness', in *PMLA*, 75 (1960), 563-70.

Valerie Minogue — '*Les Liaisons dangereuses*. A Practical Lesson in the Art of Seduction', in *The Modern Language Review*, 67 (1972), 775-86.

James S. Munro — 'Studies in Subconscious Motivation in Laclos and Marivaux', in *Studies on Voltaire and the Eighteenth Century*, LXXXIX (1972), 1153-68.

John Pappas

'Le Moralisme des *Liaisons dangereuses'*, in *Dix-huitième Siècle* , 2 (1970), 265-96.

Laclos , special number of *Revue d'Histoire littéraire de la France* , LXXXII, 4 , July-August 1982.

G.E. Rodmell

'Laclos and Stendhal', in *Studies in the French Eighteenth Century presented to John Lough* , University of Durham, 1978, pp. 173-99.

Maurice Roelens

'Le Texte et ses "conditions d'existence": l'exemple des *Liaisons dangereuses* ', in *Littérature* , 1 (February 1971), 73-81.

Jean-Luc Seylaz

'Les Mots et la chose: sur l'emploi des mots "amour", "aimer" chez Mme de Merteuil et Valmont', in above-mentioned *RHLF*, LXXXII (1982), 559-74.

Tzvetan Todorov

'Laclos et la théorie du récit', in *Tel Quel*, 27 (1966), 17-28.

R.G. Veasey

'Libertinism and the Novel', in *French Literature and its Background: 3* , *The Eighteenth Century* , ed. J. Cruickshank, London, O.U.P., 1968, pp. 148-62.